At Home on Earth

AT HOME ON EARTH

Foundations for a

Catholic Ethic of the Environment

CHARLES M. MURPHY

CROSSROAD · NEW YORK

1989

The Crossroad Publishing Company
370 Lexington Avenue, New York, N.Y. 10017

Printed in the United States of America

Library of Congress Cataloging-in-Publication Data

Murphy, Charles M.
    At home on earth : foundations for a Catholic ethic of the
environment / Charles M. Murphy.
        p.   cm.
    Bibliography: p.
    Includes index.
    ISBN 0-8245-0966-8
    1. Nature—Religious aspects—Christianity.   2. Human
ecology—Religious aspects—Christianity.   3. Catholic Church—
Doctrines.—I. Title.
BT695.5.M87   1989   89-32637
241'.691—dc20   CIP

For Natalie

CONTENTS

Foreword by Bernard Cardinal Law   ix

Preface   xi

Introduction   1
1   The Environmental Movement   30
2   Home or Hotel: An Ethic for the Earth   43
3   The Silence of Space, The Eternity of
    Time   64
4   Genesis   84
5   Genesis Applied by Pope John Paul II   106
6   Humilitas   128

Notes   145

FOREWORD

In the last few decades, humanity has become acutely aware of the fragility of our environment. Concerns are mounting all over the world about the various forms of pollution, the depletion of non-renewable sources of energy, the manipulation and destruction of natural resources, and other environmental phenomena which bring about a deterioration of the quality of life on this planet. Human responsibility for the care of our environment is inescapable. It is now imperative that we as citizens of the earth assess our culpability in terms of a careless use of our common environment, and change our patterns of behavior. The survivability of the earth and all it contains is at stake.

Ethical reflection on humanity's use of the environment has lagged behind the technological developments that have affected the ecological order. Catholic theology can serve as an invaluable resource for developing an ethical framework for human behaviour in relation to the environment. By employing a reason that is both informed by faith and guided by the authoritative teaching of the magisterium, Catholic theology is able to provide sound guidance for responsible environmental action.

In this book, Monsignor Charles Murphy takes up the task of articulating a Catholic moral vision of humanity's treatment of the environment. Monsignor Murphy is a priest of the diocese of Portland, Maine, a former rector of the North American College in Rome, and a former professor of theology at St. John's Seminary in Brighton, Massachusetts. In the pages of *At Home on Earth*, Monsignor Murphy lays the foundations for a Catholic response to the current environmental crisis. Drawing from such treasures as the book of Genesis, the work of St. Ambrose, and the teaching of Pope John Paul II, the author develops the ethical implications of the words of the prophet Isaiah, who describes God as the "designer and maker of the earth who established it, not creating it to be a waste, but designing it to be lived in" (Is 45:18).

Monsignor Murphy's "ethic of the environment" is based on the Judeo-Christian doctrine that God is the creator of the earth, and that humanity is called by God to exercise stewardship, not domination, of the earth. As stewards of creation, men and women are called to maintain and cultivate what God has given us: clean air and water, fertile land, and the beauty of nature. *At Home on Earth* is a creative contribution to an underdeveloped area of Catholic moral theology and a substantial reply to all those who are seeking ethical guidance in environmental matters.

Bernard Cardinal Law
Archbishop of Boston

PREFACE

The relations between Christianity and Western culture are long and involved. It is Christianity, accordingly, that receives credit or blame for many features of life today. One of the areas of blame is the environmental crisis.

There are those who claim that human domination and exploitation of the natural world received moral license from the biblical doctrines that humanity alone bears the divine image and was given charge to subdue and dominate the earth. Whether Christianity can be held responsible for the greed, selfishness, and short-sightedness of humanity is another question. Nonetheless, the great resources that lie within the Judaeo-Christian tradition precisely for meeting the contemporary ethical challenge of the environment have become obscured for many. They regard this tradition to be part of the problem, not the solution.

For some, Eastern religious thought holds more promise for right living on the planet. When E. F. Schumacher, for example, wrote his influential book, *Small Is Beautiful*, which had the subtitle *Economics as if*

People Mattered,[1] he had to call the chapter which applied a religious perspective to economic life "Buddhist Economics," because he felt that if he called it "Christian Economics" it would have been dismissed out of hand.

Even though we are drawing exclusively in this book upon the Bible and Christian social teaching, there is much to be learned in a complementary way from Eastern religions and their compassionate teachings concerning the ethical ideal of harmony among all creatures and the need for a purification of wants and desires as opposed to heedless consumption and endless self-gratification. It is to be expected that these Eastern cultural riches may themselves find a place within Christianity as it expands more and more into Asia. The same is to be hoped for with regard to Africa where the acculturation of Christianity to African life has made great strides.[2]

There are other factors as well that have contributed to this misunderstanding. It is to be expected that a religion based upon divine revelation would emphasize the meaning and importance of its supernatural component, on the assumption that everyone already knows about the natural world to which this revelation is addressed. But of course today the natural world itself also needs greater understanding and appreciation. The hope of heaven in a religion that holds out the promise of eternal life receives the greatest attention, but today illumination is needed as well as to how precisely this hope of heaven relates to hope for this present world and its fate. The uniqueness of the human person and human dignity and worth comprise one of the greatest legacies of the biblical view of life, but what we need to understand better is how the human person relates to the larger universe of which we are part. The need for redemption and divine grace has been a perennial theme of Christianity, but in the process the goodness and integrity of the natural world must not become lost.

It is the conviction of this writer that we are only beginning to grasp some of the environmental implications of our central Christian beliefs. The stimulus for these newer understandings of our religious heritage may be coming from our present needs and dilemmas; as I hope to demonstrate, however, these meanings are not a distortion of those beliefs but a deeper and truer understanding of them. This will become more apparent as we see these beliefs apart from ancient cultures that tended to separate the material from the spiritual realms. That tendency, although it is very common in human history, is not at all characteristic of Judaism or Christianity.

This has always been the way in history that Christian doctrines have been elaborated. The church in her councils and ordinary teachings responds to particular doctrinal controversies and expresses and defends the aspects under question. These responses, even solemn ones, do not claim to be full treatments of the issues but only to illuminate the point at hand. Thus, Augustine is rightly called *doctor gratiae*, "doctor of grace," because of his insistence over against Pelagius that natural, human efforts cannot save us, only Christ and his grace. But Augustine would not then be looked to in searching out a complete Christian doctrine regarding the environment. Neither would the polemics of the Protestant Reformation, in which the corruption of the creation and the fallenness of the world are the central concerns, be especially helpful.

I will be looking to the Book of Genesis as my principal source for an ethical foundation for the proper living of life on this planet. I will be reading it in its literal meaning, but also as it has served as an inspiration for subsequent Christian thinking about how our social relations are to be conducted. Just as the Book of Exodus has had enormous impact upon Western political thought, helping people to conceive the possibility for themselves of redemption and a better life, so, I maintain, can the Book of Genesis and an ethic based upon it provide the fertile soil for a rich appreciation of our earthly life.

Genesis was placed at the very head of the Bible, giving its stories a privileged position. These stories, colorful, surprising, and witty, ennoble both God and humans as well as all other creatures. God is portrayed there as appropriately powerful but not as remote. Humans are fittingly described as below God, but as no mere slaves, playthings, or victims. There is freedom and sovereignty on both sides. The fundamental relationship of all life to nature is firmly established, and yet there is a transcendent quality to the whole world. Above all, the stories of the creation and fall have formed the iconography of our thoughts, emotions, and values in ways that are so basic they are simply assumed. The restoration of the ceiling of the Sistine Chapel in Rome touched a common nerve; the reaching of God's creative hand to Adam's awakening hand evokes feelings about God and ourselves in a manner beyond the capacity of words to describe.

The term I use for all these insights into the meaning of our earthly life from a religious perspective is the word "home."

With strong biblical warrant from the Book of Genesis especially, the earth by divine intention at the beginning was meant to be our home. I am using "home" in contradistinction from another word to describe our earthly existence, the word "hotel." A hotel is a place only of temporary residence, for people who are traveling away from home. This is how some Christians one-sidedly have described the significance of our life on earth. This also is how many people who do not call themselves religious have experienced their lives. A hotel room is furnished with common conveniences suitable for occupancy by anonymous guests. This seems to be the operating vision for some ethicists who, apart from a religious tradition, have tried to construct the rules for our continued, shared life on this planet—minimal requirements for a life that lacks the moral density and the rich, lived-in quality of a religiously based moral code.

"Home" is the word I will use to denote the religious and moral feelings we have about the place where we live. As such, home encompasses both the supernatural and natural dimensions of our existence on earth. For the earth is to be not only our home, it is also and primarily to be the home of God. We humans have been "taken from the earth," and God has left traces of himself in a world that he not merely made but "created,"[3] as an artist creates something expressive of him/herself. And when his creation became subject to sin, in the Christian part of the story, God "humbled" himself, took on part of the earth in human form, in order to reconcile the world once again to himself.[4] The outpouring of the Holy Spirit is the end result of the work of Jesus and the guarantee that the earth will once again become the temple of God.

We are allowed, more, we are commanded, therefore, by our Christian faith to love the world and care for it.[5] Thomas Carlyle once advised an American transcendentalist, Margaret Fuller, to continue accepting the universe: "Madam, you'd better,"[6] he said. This is authentically Christian advice.

To claim the earth as home does not imply acceptance of and accommodation to all aspects of earthly life. On the contrary, to say with Genesis that at the beginning the earth was made to be God's home and ours is to set up a contrast between earthly life now and how it was intended by God. Jesus used the standard of how things were "at the beginning" to make prophetic protest against present practices. The same religious vision can serve as a mighty corrective in meeting our environmental concerns.

The doctrine of creation is a religious doctrine. It has to do with the encounter with limits, human and natural—a spiritual problem for everyone. Creation is above all a courageous affirmation about the goodness and value of our existence. It describes life as basically social. Sometimes creation is put forth and then dismissed as if it were an alternative scientific explanation of the origin of things. Creation does not purport to be a competitive theory to evolution or to have anything directly to do with "big bangs" and black holes. Creation in fact is not primarily about something that happened in the long-ago past. It has to do with the meaning of our present existence and relationships; it is intended as a guide as to how we are to live today.

Why has the environmental movement, for all its urgency, had such little impact upon the popular imagination? Why has it not changed the way we live? Perhaps it has something to do with the attempt to construct, as some environmentalists have done, an ethic out of economics or biology or some other science. Ethics, I will maintain, cannot be constructed only out of science for ethics engages the total person and not merely the mind. Perhaps, too, environmentalism has not been well served if it presents itself as a new religion, based upon a newly discovered or invented myth, for religions are not invented. The association of the environmental cause with an elitist mentality also has not helped, as if environmental concerns and social justice had to be enemies. Nature becomes a scarce good, something prestigious to own, as Lester Thurow expresses it in his book *The Zero-Sum Society:*

> . . . environmentalism is a natural product of a rising real standard of living. We have simply reached the point where, for many Americans, the next item on their acquisitive agenda is a cleaner environment. If they can achieve it, it will make all the other goods and services (boats, summer homes, and so forth) more enjoyable.[7]

No, environmentalism can only be served and helped if it makes contact with all of those who are the inheritors of the Judaeo-Christian tradition and still look to it as a source of inspiration and commitment. Only then, for many, will environmentalism take on driving force and authority. Otherwise, we are talking only to ourselves, and our gloomiest predictions about the deterioration of the planet will become self-fulfilling prophecies. We will continue to argue over policies and projects rather than over human behavior.[8]

The first part of our study, after a statement of the basic presuppositions in the introduction, is a survey both of the environmental movement and of various modern attempts, religious and secular, to develop an ethical vision large enough to encompass the whole world. The relevance of the Bible in guiding ethical decision-making will be addressed.

The middle section is devoted to a reading of the Book of Genesis as interpreted by modern biblical exegesis. St. Ambrose's homilies on the days of creation are then discussed as an example of the beginning of a Christian reflection upon the meaning of creation. Finally, we devote attention to the applications of Genesis by the present pope, John Paul II, and in particular his most recent encyclical on social concerns, *Sollicitudo rei socialis*. This encyclical draws much of its inspiration from Genesis and is a contribution on the subject of the environment within the tradition of the Catholic Church's social doctrine. That tradition relies upon revelation, but not exclusively, in meeting ethical questions. It is characteristic of Catholic social thought to give a large place to human reason, and in recent years it has sought to associate with itself the insights of all persons of whatever background. As such, that tradition, I believe, has great relevance for all who are concerned about the environment. In a concluding chapter, we will sketch an ethic that gives hope concerning our common future.

My acquaintance with John Paul comes from my years in Rome as rector of the North American College, years which overlapped the beginning period of his pontificate. Because his image in our country is colored to an extent by the controversies that have followed the Second Vatican Council, and because his writings tend to be couched in a way of thinking and speaking which are not familiar to us, his message has not had, I believe, as wide a hearing as it deserves.

I was present in St. Peter's Square the evening of October 16, 1978, when John Paul, the first Polish pope in history, stepped onto the balcony of the basilica to address the crowd after his election. His immediate reference was geographic. He spoke about coming to Rome "from a far country" to which, he did not need to add, he now could never return except as a visitor. Still, as pope, he has managed from time to time to resume the practice occasionally of hiking the hills as he once did near Cracow, and making occasional ski trips, a hint of home and a source of his spirituality and strength.

It is this side of the pope that we draw upon in this study, as well as the side of him that experienced the cost in Eastern Europe of the ideological, economic, and military rivalries that have characterized our century and which have had such an impact upon every aspect of life.

Hannah Arendt, in her thoughtful book *The Human Condition*, noted that the beginning of the space age was interpreted as introducing the possibility of escape from the "confines" of this planet. She asks, "Should the emancipation and secularization of the modern age . . . end with an even more fateful repudiation of the earth who was mother of all the living creatures under the sky?"[9]

Arendt mentions two essential characteristics of human existence that Greek antiquity ignored altogether and which are central to the Gospel, namely faith and hope. For the Greeks, she writes, "the keeping of faith was very uncommon and not too important," and as for hope, it was counted among the evils of illusion in Pandora's box. "It is this faith in and hope for the world that found perhaps its most glorious and most succinct expression in the few words with which the Gospels announced their 'glad tidings': 'A child has been born unto us.' "[10]

If the earth is worthy of being the home of God, it is worthy to be our home too.

---

* * *

My gratitude goes to a group of friends who have helped me with various aspects of this study. It has been exciting to have them as dialog partners: the Rev. Thomas Kopfensteiner, Cynthia Beckham, the Rev. Richard Clifford, S. J., the Rev. James Connor, Msgr. William Murphy, and Frank O'Hara.

INTRODUCTION

In this beginning section, I want to set forth some of the religious presuppositions employed in this study. These presuppositions need explaining, even for many religious people, because in living their religious lives they may miss these deeper implications of their own beliefs.

The first presupposition is that the earth, not someplace else, is our home. Without such a belief, committing ourselves to ensuring a livable environment for everyone would lack any real religious significance.

The ethic we seek is one whose concern embraces the whole world. Such an ethic requires an expansion of what we usually conceive as the "common good." Such a conception would entail a greater awareness of how the individual good of each part of the world we jointly inhabit, even the smallest part, must be respected. This is not just because in some way as yet unknown to us the extinction of a species, for example, may have an effect upon human welfare, but because each has a right to exist for its own sake. As Paul and Anne Ehrlich have noted, this is primarily a religious conception, for, as they

1

say, "there is no scientific way to prove that nonhuman organisms (or, for that matter, human organisms) have a right to exist."[1] From such an ethical view we will have to evolve new virtues to be cultivated, new lifestyles, a revised conception of the good life.

To grasp fully the import of the salvation which Christ brings, we must understand such salvation not as an "out-of-this-world" rescue effort, but as having very much to do with the future of all we know here on earth. Sometimes Platonist interpretations of what salvation consists of, as presented in some early Christian sources, have colored our understanding, but Platonism is basically asocial in this respect—recall its conception of life as a collection of "windowless monads." Salvation as presented in biblical sources is fundamentally social, with the fate of the individual inescapably tied up with the fate of the cosmos.

We then will indicate what we believe to be the next step in the church's still-evolving social doctrine. That doctrine already takes very seriously the good ordering of our earthly life and makes it an essential part of our religious obligations. Now that teaching must demonstrate a full commitment to environmental concerns.

Finally, and ultimately, the theological foundations for an ethic of the environment will rest upon the intuition, shared both by the professedly religious and those who do not make any such profession, that the earth is not simply our home, it is also the home of God. The earth has a spiritual quality and it is this quality that makes us care so much about its fate. Only then will what Aldo Leopold called "a land ethic" make sense,[2] "land" here referring to all natural ecosystems. I call this intuition the recovery of a "sacramental consciousness," finding in nature a sacrament of God's presence. It is he and not only ourselves to whom we must render an account of our stewardship of his creation.

THE EARTH AS HOME

There is no point to a religious ethic of the environment unless we believe that our home is on the earth and not someplace else. The thesis of this book is that the earth was created by God to be our home, as the Book of Genesis says it was, that we humans are "made of earth," that we are by nature earthly creatures and that the earth, our home, has a future that we can responsibly determine.

It is also true that any adequate religious appraisal of earthly life as we experience it must take note of the many ways that the earth is for us not a home but a place of alienation, "the land of unlikeness,"[3] in Robert Lowell's phrase, echoing Augustine. There are features of this world that are in need of saving transformation and that would cause us to declare, with the Letter to the Hebrews, that "we have here no lasting city."[4] An ethic of the environment that deserves to be called Christian therefore cannot base itself upon a romantic "back-to-nature" movement that ignores the facts of history, the positive and the negative. It must also take into account a paramount truth of Christian revelation, namely, the transcendence of the human person and his/her fundamental orientation toward communion with God.

A Christian ethic, whether of the environment or of any other aspect of our life, must be based upon the values of the coming reign of God which Jesus preached.

That reign encompasses not only the personal salvation of individual believers but of society as well, the body and the soul, the heavens and the earth. It will also mean a great reversal of much of our present earthly existence. It is true that there is a pronounced Neoplatonist influence in the way Christianity was classically formulated by the Church Fathers, an influence which tended to regard the material world as a place of temporality and therefore unreality. Such influences can be cataloged, as I will in chapter 4 in the case of St. Ambrose, but I would emphasize here that the whole direction of Christian revelation was to underscore that the kingdom's growth as not apart from the history of the world but hidden within in. At the same time it must be said that there is an inner logic in the Christian tradition whereby it is not really possible in some instances to separate out supposedly Platonist elements without neglecting important aspects of distinctively Christian doctrine. The Congregation for the Doctrine of the Faith, to give one notable example, in 1979 issued a document on certain questions related to eschatology, which saw as "indispensable" the use of a term such as "soul" to express personal survival after death before the distinct and deferred glorious manifestation of the Lord.[5]

The world for the Christian is not an illusion but God's own creation with a structure and a goodness that cannot be vitiated even by sin. The God of the creation and the God of the redemption are one, as the Creed professes: "I believe in God, the Father almighty, Creator of heaven and of earth, and in Jesus Christ his only Son our Lord, who was conceived by the Holy Spirit, born of the Virgin Mary, suffered under Pontius Pilate. . . ." The Christian faith, then, is a decidedly "worldly" faith, far too worldly for its Gnostic interpreters like Marcion who would have excised from the Bible the entire Old Testament and those parts of the New that pertained to the "inferior" creator God of the material universe.

For Marcion, Jesus the redeemer was only apparently human. What a distortion this is of Jesus of Nazareth! The Fathers clearly saw that unless Jesus were totally one of us, no one of us would be redeemed, for "what has not been assumed by God cannot be saved" (*quod non assumitur, non salvatur*). A modern visitor to the land of Jesus notes that it was along a stretch of fishing villages less than ten miles long beside the Sea of Galilee that Jesus chose most of his disciples, did most of his preaching, and performed many of his miracles. Jesus derived his parables of God's coming kingdom from this landscape and the everyday transactions of people within it; the earthiness of the parables is not at odds with but of the essence of their spiritual meaning. Jesus directs our attention not away from but toward the earth to discover God's design. "Look at the lilies of the field," Jesus declared. "Look!"[6]

The New Testament is not about heroic deeds done by royal personages, mythological happenings in the cosmos, or elevated philosophy; it is about Jesus in fields and in kitchens, in synagogues and in homes, in boats and on foot, in villages and in Jerusalem, conversing, healing, announcing God's reign with urgency. Why should Jesus not be attached to this land that he believed was given by God to his ancestor Abraham as his special portion forever? The everyday quality of what is described is its very relevance to us.

The phenomenon of religion, as we learn from the root meaning of the term, arises from the experience of "bondedness" and "connectedness" to our environment. Religion refers to the unspoken feeling of kinship and affection we humans have with our world and everything that is in it. We experience ties to the particular place where we live and we also feel at one with the universe and with its purposes. We find affinities with and reassuring responses from our fellow creatures on the planet, and we draw strength and nourishment from our natural surroundings which provide our lives with a sense of significance and of beauty. All of these experiences are brought together under the term "religion" which is basic to every human life.

The Book of Genesis, going beyond this general anthropological definition, attests that it is by God's will and design that the earth and everything that is in it have been made specifically to be our home, and that God has made us his surrogates in caring for it and tending it. "You have made us the masters over all your creatures," Psalm 8 declares; "you have put everything under our feet." We are invited by Genesis to delight with God in his creation and to find it "good."

But even more than our home, according to Genesis, the earth was made to be the home of God. He is the Creator of the heavens and the earth. It is he who at the beginning walks in its gardens in the cool of the evening. It is he who enjoys his Sabbath rest after all things are made and who invites his creatures to join him in it. It is to him that the eyes of all his creatures hopefully look, and he gives them their food in due season; he opens his hands and satisfies the desire of every living thing.[7] The beauty of the creation betrays traces of its Maker, for the "heavens declare the glory of God and all the firmament discloses his handiwork."[8] It was furthermore into this world that God's creative Word became incarnated in Christ, the temple of his glory, so that through his Spirit the whole world might become his dwelling place once more.

THE NEED FOR AN ETHIC OF THE ENVIRONMENT

In the past the development of science and the encouragement of human inventiveness were made possible by a religious belief in God's *transcendence* from his creatures having their own "objectivity." Similarly today, many believe, the religious belief in God's *immanence* within his creation as his home--even more than it is ours—can have enormous impact upon our renewed sense of respect for the world and the setting of proper ethical limits upon its human use and manipulation. To be avoided, of course, is any blurring of the distinction between God and creation as in the old pantheist heresies.

Ethics, as the tragic history of the world shows, does not arise out of logic but out of the religious imagination. It is out of the conviction that the scriptures, Church Fathers, basic Christian doctrines, and contemporary spiritual writers have much to offer in the formation of an ethical vision for the environment that I write this study.

Of the three great global issues of critical importance for the future of the world, two—the threat of nuclear annihilation and the dangerous and unjust disparities of living standards and wealth among peoples and nations—have been made the subject of pastoral letters by the bishops of the United States of America and numerous other statements of the church's magisterium. But with regard to the third global issue, namely, the environmental crisis, the U.S. bishops have declared: "Catholic social teaching on the care of the environment and the management of natural resources is still in the process of development."[9] We are in need, they state, of a "new ecological ethic" growing out of our new awareness that we share with all humanity, and I would add, for reasons given below, with all the rest of creation, a "common ecological environment."[10]

In this study, I refer to an ethic of the environment rather than an ecological ethic. Ecology is a science of the relationship between organisms and their physical and biological environments. "The environment" encompasses ecology and many other aspects of life on the planet including the social sciences as well as the life and physical sciences.

Peter Maurin, who founded with Dorothy Day the Catholic Worker movement, frequently spoke of the triad of cult, culture, and cultivation as the basic spiritual aspects of life. The Second Vatican Council itself devoted considerable attention to the first two: Its very first document concerned liturgy and its final major achievement was one largely related to human culture, but relatively little was taught regarding the cultivation of the environment. It is here that more theological reflection is required.

It is not as if, however, Catholic concern for the environment has been totally lacking. To cite only one prominent example, the late British economist Barbara Ward for many years served as a member of the Vatican's Commission on Justice and Peace and from this position called attention to the ethical concerns raised by environmental issues. Soon after the first United Nations Conference on the Human Environment, held in Stockholm in June 1972, the Vatican published Ward's reflections on the environment, *A New Creation?* In it Ward takes up the Stockholm conference's call for a "Copernican revolution" in human thinking after 400 years of scientific advances that seemed to have no limit and to be totally beneficent. A change is needed, Ward maintains, in how people look at the world, looking at it not in discreet parts and pieces but seeing instead "nature's inescapable continuum":

> They see power to be used, matter to be manipulated and do not necessarily balance short-term advantages against long-term risks. In fact, the vast power and discovery of science in the last 400 years have not been put to work by painstaking researchers who study contexts, realize linkages and see the whole process embodied in systems of interdependence. On the contrary, energy and matter have in the main been harnessed to human purposes by active, impatient, ambitious, single-minded men in pursuit of economic gain and political power and quite oblivious of the consequences of their drives. The pure love of scientific discovery may have provided most of the tools. The aims and the uses have been determined by other energies— by the worship of what Francis Bacon called "the idols of the market and the idols of the tribe."[11]

In handling the ethical questions regarding the environment, which are so complex, disciplines such as biology and economics as well as political factors have to be brought into the equation as well as theology. Some unfortunately see things only within their own specialization and make, for example, biology the supreme consideration in environmental decision-making, or economics, taken by itself. Those who would make a religion of biology might consider whatever promotes life of whatever kind, regardless of cost and other factors, to be ethically positive. Others, equivalently making a religion out of economics, might attempt to put dollar values on a natural resource such as a national park or on a human activity such as fishing. What people are willing to pay to go to a park, use it and maintain it, constitutes for them the park's true worth. To take another example, the preservation of an endangered species such as the famous snail darter could, depending upon your point of view, have the highest ethical priority or no priority at all. Some would regard anything less than a pristine condition to be ethically deficient, and yet, in the modern industrialized world and given political realities, a pristine air quality, for example, might be an absolute necessity for a park, but a lower level might be ethically acceptable for a city.

A Christian ethical analysis would have to balance the private rights of individuals with what is called, technically, "the common good." Such an approach will have heavy going because of a long legal and cultural history in the English-speaking world which attaches an unquestioned importance to the value of private ownership of property justly acquired. Going back to feudal times and firmly embedded in our own Constitution, the right of private property has been made a basic human right, and a primary function of government is considered to be giving this right proper protection. A

Christian ethical reflection goes against the absoluteness of such a right and asserts private ownership to be legitimate but strictly conditioned. The earth and everything that is in it belong to themselves and to God before they belong to anyone else.

The moral issues surrounding the privatization of what are called the public commons were given sharp focus in an article written by Garret Hardin and entitled "The Tragedy of the Commons."

Hardin, a professor of biology, claims there are certain human problems that fall into the category of "no technical solution possible"—that is to say, their solution is not to be found in the natural sciences but in a revolution of morals. One such human dilemma is the arms race, the dilemma of steadily increasing military power and steadily decreasing national security. "If the great powers continue to look for solutions in the area of science and technology only," the scientists Wiesner and York assert, "the result will be to worsen the situation."[12]

To counter the prevailing "invisible-hand" theory of how the common good will be served by people pursuing only their private claims and interests, Hardin proposes another conception, one called "the tragedy of the commons." Adam Smith in *The Wealth of Nations* popularized the notion of the "invisible hand," that an individual who intends only his own gain is led by an invisible hand to promote the public interest. Hardin comments that Smith did not assert that his theory was invariably true, but his ideas gave credibility to the tendency we have to assume that decisions reached individually will, in fact, be the best for the entire society. The rebuttal to the invisible hand lies in the well-documented "tragedy of the commons," that is, the ruin that comes to a limited space brought about by a public exercising unrestrained freedom. "Maritime nations," for example, "still respond automatically to the shibboleth of the 'freedom of the seas.' Professing to believe in the 'inexhaustible resources of the oceans,' they bring species after species of fish and whales closer to extinction."[13] The tragedy of the commons with regard to air and water may be seen in the problem of pollution caused by a particular concept of private property which carries with it the right to do with the property as the owner sees fit.

Occasionally public ownership of the commons is put forth as the best guarantee against private misuse, but even here the guarantee may not be so secure. Public ownership of large areas of the United States has created new commercial possibilities through government leases for oil exploration, mining operations, and tree-cutting that has devastated ancient forests, not to mention the military uses of these lands as nuclear test sites.

The definition of the common good and commitment to it are not easy to achieve in the modern context, as Daniel Maguire explains in his book *A New American Justice*. The common good is not just a utilitarian goal, "the greatest good for the greatest number," for the good of the majority can mean great injustice to the minorities left behind. The common good brings with it a notion of community life involving everyone and everything without exception, living in mutual accommodation. It transcends even national boundaries. Its scope is as large as the earth itself.[14]

The particular problem of the commons that Hardin addresses in his article is that of uncontrolled population growth, a problem clearly related to concern for limited natural resources. In 1968, Pope Paul VI addressed this problem in his much-discussed encyclical *Humanae vitae* ("On Human Life"). While endorsing the principle of "responsible parenthood," that is, of not heedlessly bringing into the world children beyond our capacity to care for them, Paul received enormous criticism for teaching that there is "an inseparable connection between sexual union and procreation" which is not to be destroyed by human intervention. This was considered to be the height of moral irresponsibility by certain of the pope's critics, but from an environmental perspective his encyclical takes on a much more favorable light. Instead of an automatic endorsement of new methods of artificial contraception, the pope insisted we "acknowledge ourselves not to be the arbiter of the sources of human life, but rather the ministers of the design established by the Creator."[15] The pope continues: "The church is the first to praise and recommend the intervention of intelligence in a function which so closely associates the rational creature with his Creator; but the church affirms that this must be done with respect for the order established by God."[16]

The pope's concern, however, extended beyond the breaking of the bond between the use of sex and fertility. He likewise wished to safeguard a human activity which is a personal expression of love from the intrusion of governmental and scientific "authorities." He asked:

> Who will stop rulers from favoring, from even imposing upon their peoples, if they were to consider it necessary, the method of contraception which they judge to be most efficacious? In such a way, human beings, wishing to avoid individual, family, or social

difficulties encountered in the observance of the divine law, would reach the point of placing at the mercy of the intervention of public authorities the most personal and most reserved sector of conjugal intimacy.[17]

An environmentalist, writing out of his own context and concern, sharply brings into focus the logical connection between separating sex and fertility and the exploitation of the planet:

There is an uncanny *resemblance* between our behavior toward each other and our behavior toward the earth. Between our relation to our own sexuality and our relation to the reproductivity of the earth, for instance, the resemblance is plain and strong and apparently inescapable. By some connection that we do not recognize, the willingness to exploit one becomes the willingness to exploit the other. The conditions and the means of exploitation are likewise similar. The modern failure of marriage that has so estranged the sexes from each other seems analogous to the "social mobility" that has estranged us from our land, and the two are historically parallel. It may even be argued that these two estrangements are very close to being one, both of them having been caused by the disintegration of the household, which was the formal bond between marriage and the earth, between human sexuality and its sources in the sexuality of creation.[18]

What is technologically possible, what is economically advantageous, what is demographically demonstrable, and every other partial perspective on life must be weighed in the balance and given objective moral evaluation even if such an evaluation seems to inhibit "progress." The ethical question to be resolved is actually what truly constitutes progress.

THE CHRISTIAN AND THE SALVATION OF THE WORLD

There is of course an unavoidable ambiguity the Christian feels about "the world." First, there is the "world as we know it,"[19] the world of sin and death, the world for which Jesus "does not pray"[20] for it is "passing away." "Do not be conformed to this world," St. Paul admonishes. The Second Vatican Council interprets "world" in this passage to mean "a spirit of vanity and malice whereby human activity is distorted from being ordered to the service of God and humanity to being an instrument of sin."[21] Then there is the world that is the human world, the whole human family, to whom, according to the recently issued apostolic exhortation of John Paul II on the laity, "the mission of the church is more directly concerned," with "the aim of making it more aware of its vocation to *communio* with God."[22] It is with regard to this human world that the exhortation interprets the passage, "For God so loved the world that he gave his only Son, that whoever believes in him should not perish but have eternal life."[23] Finally there is a third meaning to "world" which is understood to comprise the immense reality of creation of which humanity is but a part and over which we humans are to exercise dominion. It is about the organization of the life of the world understood in the third sense—with respect to its continuance, proper care, and enhancement[24]—that we must speak in developing the theological foundations for an ethic of the environment as we propose to do in this study.

The world is in need of salvation, a salvation that comes from Christ. A one-sided emphasis upon our pilgrim status in this passing world and upon the priority of contemplation over action, however, sometimes is misinterpreted in the most harmful and irresponsible manner as seeming to remove the Christian from becoming an actor and contributor in the world's fate. This tendency the Second Vatican Council specifically wished to address when it taught that far from removing responsibility for the world from the Christian's concern, religious faith gives that responsibility an even stronger motivation.[25] The church exists, the council taught, as a "sacrament for the salvation of the world."[26] As members of the church, Christians are to apply the saving results of Christ's redemption to the whole created world which still bears the effects of sin. In this way they become God's own partners in carrying out his ongoing creation and recreation of the world.[27]

But there is another latent danger in the stress upon "this passing world" improperly understood and that is the belief, professed by some contemporary fundamentalists, that the whole material world is going to be destroyed anyway, so why bother about it? This belief was found to be at the basis of the psychology of workers in plants making neutron bombs who could tranquilly contemplate the world's destruction by such bombs because it fit their theological view that everything according to the Bible is going to be blown away while the true believers will be raptured into another world.[28]

The apocalyptic imagery of the atomic bomb was employed with great visual effect by Stanley Kubrick in his film *Dr. Strangelove*. The playwright David Rabe calls the mushroom cloud our "communal nightmare totem" in an appreciative piece regarding Kubrick's work:

> The experience of first seeing Mr. Kubrick's *Dr. Strangelove* rushing to its conclusion is fixed in my mind. It was in a state of near hysteria that I watched the great white plumes of flowering nuclear devastation erupting in gyres one upon the other and heard the eerie, innocent music in the background, the tune being sung by innocuous voices in their sweet but dopey harmony: "We'll meet again, don't know where, don't know when, but I know we'll meet again some sunny day." With the cataclysms depicted in the rather abstract beauty of their fury, the image that we had emerged from the 50's sharing as our communal nightmare totem, the mushroom cloud, appeared again and again, a kind of exploding cross when you really looked at it, the plume intersected by the light rushing out in either direction; and with the sappy, nostalgic music beneath it, a kind of cozy, ostensibly sweet, yet somehow lifeless, invitation to a universal and final rendezvous, it seemed to me some dark yet cherished longing of our hearts had been unmistakably depicted.[29]

The material world thus becomes only a backdrop against which the drama of human salvation is played out and then falls back into the nothingness from which it was created. It has no place in the heavenly kingdom. Such a view, as we will see, is contradicted by the church's growing realization of the implications of her own distinctive beliefs about God's creation of the material world and his satisfaction with it, the incarnation of Christ, his bodily resurrection, and the promise of "a new heaven and a new earth."

The promised salvation in Christian tradition in fact becomes trivialized if it is thought of as merely an out-of-this-world survival of individual souls after death. Certainly in the faith of Israel, the fate of the individual person is inseparable from the fate of the entire people, a corporate reality and a corporate salvation. It is difficult as well, within the Judaeo-Christian scheme, to imagine how the physical world would not in some way participate in the promised resurrection, considering the fact that humanity and nature form together one unified universe.

The "end" of the world, therefore, must be understood not as the ceasing to be of everything except immortal souls, as in Neoplatonism, but in the sense that the word "finis" or end has in Latin, namely, that the world is to achieve finally the goal and purpose God assigned to it when he first created it.

In the religious revolution that Christianity brought about, the world is our mediation of God. There is for Christians, as Karl Rahner has pointed out, no separate, sacred realm where God is to be found.[30] Those who worship the Father, the true worshipers whom the Father seeks, Jesus declared, are those who worship neither upon sacred mountains nor in sacred temples, but "in spirit and in truth."[31] The first Christian churches, accordingly, were private homes, and then, eventually, in large urban centers such as Rome, basilicas—large public meeting halls. Pagans were not admitted into the tiny precincts of their temples where the gods dwelt and only the priests entered. Christians entered their places of prayer by right, as sons and daughters of God whom they addressed not bowed to the ground but in a dignified standing position.[32]

Worldlessness as a Christian ideal, it must be admitted, has been proposed by Tertullian and others, especially in the monastic tradition, but Hannah Arendt justly cites this as an example of the various and contradictory repercussions of a revelatory event of the magnitude of Christ's birth, an event which in its paramount meaning represents the highest affirmation possible of the value of belonging to this world. The monastic vocation has always been regarded not as the normative but the exceptional expression of Christian life as pointing beyond this world to its final consummation.

Eric Voegelin would argue that Gnosticism, which he defines as a state of alienation from reality and an extracosmic isolation of existential consciousness, was a derailment from the Gospel. He writes:

> The strength of the Gospel is its concentration on the one point that is all-important: that the truth of reality has its center not in the cosmos at large, not in nature or society or imperial rulership, but in the presence of the Unknown God in human existence. . . . This very strength, however, can cause a breakdown if the emphasis on the center of truth becomes so intense that its relations to the reality of which it is the center are neglected or inter-

rupted. . . . In that case, however, there is not a process of revelation-history, nor a millennial movement culminating in the epiphany of the Son of God, but only the eruption of an extracosmic God into a cosmos. Since the revelation of this extra-cosmic God is the only truth that existentially matters, the cosmos, its gods and its history, become a reality with the index of existential untruth.[33]

Justin Martyr sees the *logos* of the Gospel as the same Word of the same God as the *logos spermatikos* of philosophy, but at a later state of manifestation in history. Justin does not regard Christianity as an alternative to philosophy. "Note above all," Voegelin concludes, "the difficulty the Church has with its own believers who want to be Christians at the price of their own humanity." Voegelin interprets John 12:44 ("I am the light which has come into the cosmos not to judge but to save") to mean that the cosmos is not a habitat from which our lives have to be rescued for eternity: on the contrary, the inhabitants are not to be evacuated but saved in the drama of existence.[34]

Whatever we may think about these elaborate speculations on the part of Voegelin, there is an unmistakable human tendency to regard as more "spiritual" abstractions from everyday existence in the material universe. Spirituality thus has a tendency to become a separate or even esoteric zone rather than a quality of existence itself, something already mysteriously "there" and ready to be discovered, like the treasure Jesus speaks about that is buried in a field that someone happens to stumble upon. Such a discovery always comes, as Jesus says, as a piece of surprising "good news."[35] This spiritualizing tendency may also have much to do with the failure to recognize the environment and its preservation as a spiritual issue. The Second Vatican Council identified the separation of faith from life as one of the greatest errors of our age.[36]

THE NEXT STEP IN THE CHURCH'S SOCIAL TEACHING

This study carries forward the work I did in my doctoral dissertation which explored the relationship between the preaching of the Gospel and action in the world on behalf of justice. That relationship was described by the World Synod of Bishops convened in Rome in 1971 as "constitutive": that is, working for justice is not merely a secondary or optional element in the Gospel but pertains to its very meaning. Charity has always been considered a field of activity for the church, but, as the synod pointed out, there can be no real charity without justice, for doing justice is charity's first demand.[37]

This affirmation about the relationship between the Gospel and justice has been considered a high point of the church's social doctrine as it has developed over the past century. It sharply brought into focus the "historicity" of Christ's saving actions in bringing about the possibility of a better life even here on earth for everyone. Concern for the environment is a logical extension of these insights.

At the 1971 synod, the discussion was not yet about "liberation theology" which later came into prominence. The argument about the church's action on behalf of justice revolved around charges of "excessive horizontalism," that is, the danger that the divine offer of eternal salvation which is the Gospel might be understood as merely another social action scheme to be achieved by human means. The "vertical" element in the Gospel, its connection with God and his grace, which is its very "originality," would thus become compromised. Similar concerns will have to be met as the church develops an ethic for the environment. Our eternal home in heaven will have to be seen as the very future of our home on earth. That future will be a gift of grace and the end result of Christ's redemption, but human responsibility and freedom in the care of the planet are not thus declared irrelevant. All the wisdom and intelligence at our disposal will have to be brought into play in seeking solutions which have been given by God to human responsibility and agency to achieve.

Harold J. Berman has situated the legal beginnings of the church's direct concern about the right ordering of secular affairs with the reforms of Pope Gregory VII in the eleventh century. The church's intent was to protect her own freedom and independence as a spiritual entity accountable only to God, but the net result of these reforms was a theological and legal separation of powers between church and state. The state was recognized as having competency to manage its own affairs, but the church, as guardian of the divine and natural laws, retained the right to judge whether the laws of the state were in conformity with these higher decrees; if they were not, citizens were not held bound to them. And even though there was a separation of powers, in addition to the common moral authority of the church, there was one community of believers who transcended national boundaries.

Berman cites this history to show how really impoverished we are in dealing with a worldwide moral issue such as the environment. We have, Berman contends, no common moral authority, for the church is now considered a private option of individuals. We have no international community of persons comprising the entire Western world. Even our legal traditions have become so specialized and nationalized, Berman argues, that we are startled to learn that most of our legal institutions did not originate in the modern world but were put in place in the Middle Ages. This gets us into all kinds of trouble—for example, in understanding such things as property rights that, wrested out of their grounding in more ancient and Christian legal precedents, which situated and circumscribed them within a range of social responsibilities, have been made sacrosanct in themselves,[38] subject only to the will of their owners.

The modern phase of the church's social doctrine was inaugurated by Pope Leo XIII in 1891 and his encyclical *Rerum novarum* ("Of New Things").[39] It was a cry of protest against the human cost of rapid industrialization and in favor of workers' rights. More than that, it was the beginning of a major effort by the church to resist being moved to the sidelines of world affairs. As that teaching developed, the church more and more saw her role as the defender of human rights, of all that is human. Now she must see herself as the defender of the natural world as well.

The church/state dichotomy, described as two perfect societies existing side-by-side and sometimes in mutual competition, was succeeded but not abandoned by another way of expressing the church's concern for secular matters, and that was in terms of church/world. This was

the way the Second Vatican Council in its pastoral constitution on "The Church in the World of Today" (*Gaudium
et spes*) phrased the relationship. The church, the council
taught, shares the common fate and history of the world,
and to these common problems the church comes not to
dominate but to serve and to make her own unique
contribution. Here is the key passage from *Gaudium et
spes:*

> The church, at once a visible organization and a
> spiritual community, travels the same journey as all
> humankind and shares the same earthly lot with
> the world: it is to be the leaven and, as it were, the
> soul of human society in its renewal by Christ and
> transformation into the family of God.
>
> That the earthly and the heavenly city penetrate
> one another is a fact open only to the eyes of faith;
> moreover, it will remain the mystery of human
> history, which will be harassed by sin until the
> perfect revelation of the splendor of the sons of God.
> In pursuing its own salvific purpose not only does
> the church communicate divine life to humanity
> but in a certain sense it casts the reflected light of
> that divine life over all the earth, notably in the way
> it heals and elevates the dignity of the human per-
> son, in the way it consolidates society, and endows
> the daily activity of human beings with a deeper
> sense and meaning. The church then believes it can
> contribute much to humanizing the human family
> and its history through each of its members and its
> community as a whole.
>
> Furthermore, the Catholic church gladly values
> what other Christian churches and ecclesial com-
> munities have contributed and are contributing co-

operatively to the realization of this aim. Similarly it
is convinced that there is a considerable and varied
help that it can receive from the world in preparing
the ground for the Gospel, both from individuals
and from society as a whole, by their talents and
activity.[40]

That "ground for the Gospel" which the council
speaks about needs to encompass not only human society
but the whole natural world. This is the next step for the
social teaching of the church to take.

The case of animals being considered, like the land,
merely human property is a case in point. A standard
Catholic manual of moral theology much in use until
recently categorized animals under three headings: domesticated, confined, and wild. The domesticated simply
belong to their human owners. The confined, such as
doves and bees, likewise are the property of those making
use of them. As for the wild animals, it is simply a case of
finders, keepers. Experiments upon animals have been
justified if from them there is some prospect of beneficial
effect upon human life and health. Cruelty to animals
was rejected on the moral grounds that such behavior is
demeaning to human beings.[41]

Animal-rights advocates reject such views as human
supremacist. Some do not want animals used for human
food or for any other human use such as in laboratory
experiments, fur coats, hunting, circuses, or zoos. If
human rights are to prevail over the rights of animals
simply because humans are smarter, they argue, do humans of subnormal intelligence for this reason have less
rights?[42]

As we will see below when we examine the meaning

of the Book of Genesis, the uniqueness of the human person is not based upon intelligence but has a religious ground. That religious ground has very much to do with humanity's being given the charge by God to care for his creation. This belief could form the basis for a whole new moral valuation regarding nonhuman life.

A SACRAMENTAL CONSCIOUSNESS

Western society with its industry and technology has had a great impact upon the world's ecosystem and is identified by the rest of the world as "the future." In the West secularization is also far advanced: It is a society which for various reasons has lost what could be called its sacramental consciousness—that is, of nature and the events of human life as speaking to us of God. The recovery of a vibrant sacramental life, even in a highly industrialized, technological society, holds the key, I believe, to the environmental challenge at hand.

The very transcendence of God from creation, a hallmark of the Judaeo-Christian tradition, has had the effect of demythologizing nature, making it an autonomous, secular zone. Our religious tradition itself, therefore, has allowed us to regard nature as the object of scientific examination and human progress. But a totally profane world is a modern conception. For the religious person, in any age, nature is never just "nature" but retains a sacred quality as "creation," something made and sustained by God. Nature as creation is a sacrament, a visible representation of God, to whom it ultimately belongs.[43]

Even Christianity itself, in its contemporary experience, manifests, according to Mircea Eliade, a sacramental life that is "gravely impoverished." He writes:

> As for the Christianity of the industrial societies and especially the Christianity of intellectuals, it has long since lost the cosmic values that it still possessed in the Middle Ages. The cosmic liturgy, the mystery of nature's participation in the Christological drama, have become inaccessible to Christians living in a modern city. . . . At most, we recognize that we are responsible not only to God but also to history—the world no longer is felt as the work of God.[44]

The Church Fathers, Eliade continues, found correspondences not only between the two Testaments but also impressive mutual illuminations between human history, the history of Christ, and the world of nature. Christian baptism, for example, the initiatory sacrament of rebirth, is inextricably bound up with Christ's saving death and resurrection, but never is this new valorization seen to contradict the universally disseminated aquatic symbolism woven into life on earth. *Nothing is missing:* Noah and the flood of the Old Testament, Christ himself, baptism—all are counterparts of the watery element which dissolves old forms, cleanses and nourishes. Paul Tillich, who in his lifetime did so much to revive a renewed sacramental consciousness within Protestantism, frequently spoke of the power of sacraments. For him, it did not matter whether there be two sacraments as in most Protestant traditions, or seven as in the numeration of the Council of Trent; what mattered was a

sacramental sense of life. In his sermon entitled, "Nature
Mourns for a Lost God," Tillich declares:

> Let me ask you a question: are we still able to
> understand what a sacrament means? The more we
> are estranged from nature, the less we can answer
> affirmatively. That is why, in our time, the sacra-
> ments have lost much of their significance for indi-
> viduals and churches. For in the sacraments, nature
> participates in the process of salvation, bread and
> wine, water and light, and all the great elements of
> nature become the bearers of spiritual meaning and
> saving power. Natural and spiritual powers are
> united—reunited—in the sacrament.[45]

Marguerite Yourcenar, the first woman member of
the prestigious Academie Française, recalled that her
religious formation in Europe at the beginning of the
century seemed to force her to choose between the
Catholic religion and the universe. Her choice was easy. "I
preferred the universe," she writes. "At that time these
two aspects of the sacred—religion and the universe—
seemed incompatible. One seemed far more comprehensive than the other. The church hid the forest from
view. . . . I have no difficulty imagining a Catholic capable of combining the two . . . but in the rather attenu-
ated Catholicism of the turn of the century such a thing
was scarcely possible."[46]

A more authentic spiritual life, one that is more
sacramental, rooted in the earth, is crucial not only for
religion itself but also for the future of the planet. G. K.
Chesterton had it right when he wrote:

. . . the mystic comes and says that a green tree symbolizes life. It is not so. Life symbolizes a green tree. Just in so far as we get into the abstract, we get away from the reality, we get away from the mystery, we get away from the tree.[47]

"Mystery" is the Greek-derived synonym for sacrament, its Latin equivalent. It refers to something hidden that is to be revealed, but that something is not strange or unfamiliar. It is in fact something very congenial. When we experience it, we say "Yes."[48]

The mystery hidden from the ages that is now revealed is that God was in Christ reconciling the world to himself. It is a mystery that is expressed in the eucharistic sacrament and is related to the sacramentality of the universe itself. These sacramental moments are anticipations, present signs of the kingdom's coming. Anne Morrow Lindbergh discovered in five shells collected on the shore clues both to the meaning of her life and to the meaning of the planet. "We find again," she writes in her classic book of meditations, *Gift from the Sea*, "some of the joy in the now, some of the peace in the here, some of the love in me and thee which go to make up the kingdom of heaven on earth."[49]

1 THE ENVIRONMENTAL MOVEMENT

In some ways environmentalism reached its apex the day it began—Earth Day, April 22, 1970—and steadily declined in popular interest ever since. It was called "the birthday of a new ethic,"[1] one that abandons the mores of the frontier and recognizes that modern, highly developed societies are inescapably bound to a fragile ecosystem of land, water, and air, and 20 million or more Americans assembled in public rallies for its cause; a scant five years later, 100 devotees came together in Manhattan for the observance. The presidentially proclaimed "Decade of the Environment" concluded with none of its ambitious goals achieved even after the expenditure of billions of dollars. In other ways, however, the environmental movement raised issues that would not go away regardless of rising and flagging public and political interest and no matter how grossly underestimated was the intractableness of the problems to be faced.

The environmental cause, from the beginning, was to an extent the special enthusiasm of a privileged and affluent minority who wished to preserve their particular lifestyle even if it meant impeding the further development of natural resources in other parts of the world, which presumably would be kept in poverty to satisfy the preservationist agenda. But it was also the environmental movement that identified and dramatized concerns so fundamental and so pervasive that they touched every level of society and every corner of the globe. An enlightening study could be made, to cite one example close to my own home, of the public testimony given by so many and with such fervor to register their emphatic "No!" to the federal government which had contemplated in 1986–87 a nuclear waste dump in the state of Maine. Such a study would demonstrate not only how wide and deep was the popular feeling about such a proposal but would also bring to light how much the psyches of the speakers were attached to the landscape—the rivers, the mountains, the coastlands. The very meaning of their lives, their mental well-being, their sense of the divine, their hope for immortality emerged, however inarticulately, in these public gatherings.

New phrases have entered the language as the result of environmental concerns, phrases like the much-abused "quality of life," which has become a cliché and masks alarming imprecision of thought even as it is being invoked as a guiding concept to determine such profound questions as who shall live and who shall die.

Walker Percy, the physician-turned-novelist, has a good time in *The Thanatos Syndrome* spoofing the whole idea. The novel features a mad physician who is proposing the transfer of all infants who are candidates for pedeuthanasia by reason of retardation, Down's syndrome, AIDS infection, gross malformation, etc.—in other words, "who have no chance for a life of any sort of acceptable quality"[2]—from the so-called "Qualitarian

Center" to a hospice, where they will mercifully be allowed to die. Such nightmarish visions certainly show the need for a more adequate ethical approach.

There is then an unavoidable ambiguity, some would say artificiality, about the environmental movement that has caused many who are concerned and thoughtful about these issues to keep their distance. Adding to the ambiguity have been the doomsday scenarios that predicted imminent "ecotastrophe" if present trends in population, food production, industrialization, and resource depletion continued, predictions that soon proved to be grossly overstated and some of which were even to be reversed. A conference on "The Limits of Growth" sponsored by the Club of Rome in 1972 had made many such predictions but then called for *faster* economic growth in Third World countries to help close the gap between rich and poor cultures.

The environmental question has been politicized by Greenpeace, which, in Europe, has fielded its own candidates for public office on a platform that has caused unease because of its antiestablishment tone: antimilitary, antigovernment, and some would say, antihistory. Greenpeace leapt into prominence with its vigorous advocacy of protection for whales, but in its later evolution has staged dramatic protests against nuclear testing, for example, in the South Pacific. The sinking of the *Rainbow Warrior* in Auckland created much publicity and also much controversy over Greenpeace's aims and tactics. At the same time, real political gains on environmental issues have been achieved worldwide; few today can claim ignorance of the need for environmental impact assessments before any major project is undertaken.

If we were to chart the brief history of the environmental movement, we might divide it into two phases of which the earlier could be called "optimistic conservationism" and the later, "pessimistic environmentalism."

OPTIMISTIC CONSERVATIONISTS

Before there was conservationism there was the "naturalism" of Henry David Thoreau and Ralph Waldo Emerson who, in the tradition of Jean-Jacques Rousseau, advocated the religious and therapeutic values of contact with nature untrammeled by human industry and alteration. This basically romantic approach, which was to reemerge in the environmental movement of the 1960's, does not characterize the conservationists who at the turn of the century launched the great protests against exploitation by miners, ranchers, and loggers. The conservationists frequently spoke about stewardship of the land and its resources, but they really were advocates of multiuse development of America's vast landmass and were robustly optimistic that development would prove no enemy of their conservationism.

Outdoorsmen like President Theodore Roosevelt saw nothing wrong with pairing development and conservation. America's first great conservationist, John Muir (1838–1914), the founder of the Sierra Club, broke with Roosevelt over the issue of public works in the Yosemite and Sequoia National Parks then being established.

Frederick Law Olmsted was the first to conceive of the idea of a national park, the idea that a deserving place simply not be for sale. Muir went on to create through his writings a constituency for the national-park and the conservation cause. "Everybody needs beauty as well as bread," Muir wrote in *The Yosemite*, "places to play in and pray in, where nature may heal and cheer and give strength to the body and soul alike. . . . Nevertheless, like anything else worthwhile, from the very beginning, however well guarded, they have always been subject to attack by despoiling gainseekers and mischiefmakers of every degree from Satan to senators, eagerly trying to make everything immediately and selfishly commercial, with schemes disguised in smug-smiling philanthropy, industriously, sham-piously crying, 'Conservation, conservation, panutilization.' "[3]

Recent reassessments of the conservation movement see it as a phenomenon of an educated elite and the outgrowth of new scientific fields of inquiry such as forestry, geology, and water treatment, rather than a grass-roots enterprise.

The beginnings of a deeper, ethical approach to the land can be seen in the writings of Aldo Leopold (1886–1948), a founder of the Wilderness Society. Leopold is most widely remembered as the author of "The Land Ethic," which appears as a chapter of his book *A Sand County Almanac*, published the year of his death. Human life for Leopold has a fundamental "land-relationship" demanding an ethic of its own. "That land is a community is the basic concept of ecology, but that land is to be loved and respected is an extension of ethics," he wrote.[4]

It is now commonly accepted that respect for the human person does not permit anyone to become the property of another. There is a developing social ethic to regulate relations among communities of persons and even nations. But Leopold adds, "there is as yet no ethic dealing with [humanity's] relation to land. . . . Land is still property. The land-relation is still strictly economic, entailing privileges but not obligations."[5]

Leopold therefore saw the conservation movement as the "embryo," to use his term, of a future land ethic, a necessary third step in ethical sophistication after the development of the ethics of individual life and of social relations. "The proof that conservation has not yet touched these foundations of conduct," he wrote, "lies in the fact that philosophy and religion have not yet heard of it."[6] Leopold was convinced that once these issues were addressed a new land ethic would come into being.

Leopold's confidence has proven unjustified. Years after he wrote, it has been commented that "a land ethic simply does not exist in the United States of America."[7] The complexity of cooperative mechanisms has increased with population density and with the efficiency of tools. It was simpler, for example, to define antisocial uses of sticks and stones in the days of the mastodons than of bullets and billboards in the age of motors.[8]

No doubt because conservationism was a phenomenon of Protestant, capitalist America, it was untouched by the long Christian tradition going back to the Church Fathers that the right to private ownership can never be an absolute right since the earth is the Lord's and what belongs to God belongs to all. Greed and acquisitiveness beyond personal need were the special targets of the preaching of the Fathers as posing particular danger to eternal salvation. The right to private ownership of the land or anything else, according to this rich tradition of thought, is strictly conditioned by what is called the irrevocable "universal destination" of all things. Some of the implications of this teaching can be startling to modern Christian ears; for example, if someone lacks the necessities of life and his/her neighbor has a surplus, he/she may appropriate what is needed to sustain life, and this in no sense is to be regarded as stealing, even if the surplus being appropriated was originally acquired by legitimate means.

This is how the Second Vatican Council summarized traditional teaching regarding "earthly goods and their universal destination":

> God destined the earth and all it contains for all individuals and peoples so that all created things would be shared fairly by all mankind under the guidance of justice tempered by charity. No matter what the structures of property are in different peoples, according to various and changing circumstances and adapted to their lawful institutions, we must never lose sight of this universal destination of earthly goods. In his/her use of things, every person should regard external goods he/she legitimately owns not merely as exclusive to him/herself, but common to others also, in the sense that they can benefit others as well as him/herself. Therefore every person has the right to possess a sufficient amount of the earth's goods for him/herself and his/her family. This has been the opinion of the Fathers and Doctors of the Church, who taught that we are bound to come to the aid of the poor and to do so not merely out of our superfluous goods. When a person is in extreme necessity he/she has the right to supply him/herself with what he/she needs out of the riches of others.[9]

As we will discuss in chapter 5, what belongs to God not only belongs to all human beings but also belongs to itself and to all the other creatures with which we share this planet.

PESSIMISTIC ENVIRONMENTALISTS

Many dire predictions about the future of the planet culminated in Earth Day 1970, which introduced the "environmental decade." Rachel Carson in 1962 wrote her influential *Silent Spring* in which she contended that unless DDT and other pesticides and herbicides were banned from use, the planet would be unfit for all life. Our springs would be "silent," Carson dramatically predicted, because all the birds that are part of the foodchain affected by the toxins would likewise fall victim. A key passage from *Silent Spring* is the following:

> Along with the possibility of the extinction of mankind by nuclear war, the central problem of our age has therefore become the contamination of man's total environment with such substances that accumulate in the tissues of plants and animals and even penetrate the germ cells to shatter or alter the very material of heredity upon which the shape of the future depends. . . . It is ironic to think that man might determine his own future by something so seemingly trivial as the choice of an insect spray. All this has been risked—for what? Future historians may well be amazed by our distorted sense of proportion. How could intelligent beings seek to control a few unwanted species by a method that contaminated the entire environment and brought

the threat of disease and death even to their own kind? Yet this is precisely what we have done. . . . All this is not to say there is no insect problem and no need of control. I am saying rather, that control must be geared to realities, not mythical situations and that the methods employed must be such that they do not destroy us along with the insects.[10]

Silent Spring is still in print twenty-five years later and over 2 million copies have been sold.

What was called "the population bomb" relentlessly ticking away posed still another danger, according to others, of no less magnitude. Famines in the 1970's were predicted as inevitable unless population trends were turned around immediately.

Despite the gloom, many positive steps were taken. The 1970 National Environmental Policy Act changed the way in which government agencies made their decisions. The act required that environmental considerations be included and weighed appropriately along with economic, social, and other factors in government planning and action. "Detailed statements" (the now-famous environmental impact statements) had to be drawn up to assess the potential effects upon the environment of all proposed "major" federal government actions. The term "human" environment was used to distinguish these new considerations from political and economic factors.

Procedures began to be set up to do the called-for evaluations. In December of the same year, President Nixon created the U. S. Environmental Protection Agency (E.P.A.). A variety of laws were passed in the 1970's and 1980's to address substantive aspects of environmental law. Among these were the Clean Air Act, the Clean

Water Act, the Toxic Substance Control Act, and the Resource Conservation and Recovery Act (solid waste management)—all during the 1970's. In 1980, the Comprehensive Environmental Response, Compensation, and Liability Act established a "superfund" to provide for toxic-waste cleanup.

Two other types of statutes had to do with species protection and so-called "special-area" protection, some of these going back to early in the century. Among the species-protection laws were those regarding endangered species, marine mammal protection, fishery conservation, migratory-bird conservation, and bald-eagle protection. The "special-area" legislation encompassed the Wild and Scenic Rivers Act, the National Forest Management Act, the Wilderness Act, and the National Wildlife Refuge System Administration Act.

U. S. aid abroad originally was exempt from the environmental regulations imposed domestically, but now the Agency for International Development (A.I.D.) must operate under rules that are in some respects more stringent than those applying within the United States. Particular emphasis has been given to tropical forests and other "fragile" areas subject to extreme development pressures.

Later federal legislation addressed the protection of endangered species, the transportation of hazardous materials, the production of toxins, and the regulation of strip mining. But as the "environmental decade" progressed, economic problems, enormously high costs, and the very difficulty of the problems being addressed caused a downturn in environmental fortunes. Earth Day 1970, according to some, represented an expensive overreaction. The much hailed 55 mile-an-hour speed limit

was being reversed and pollution controls on new auto-
mobiles were being eased to help a troubled industry.
Some accused environmentalists of playing nature
against people and jobs.[11] In retrospect, the search for
environmental quality was seen to be due, at least in
part, to the rising standard of living of its comparatively
well-off advocates.

We find ourselves at the point in the brief evolution of
environmentalism when goals have been cut back in the
interest of realism, but also when progress is being made
by moving away from a mere series of unrelated pollu-
tion-control laws and animal-protection laws, all enacted
on a substance-by-substance or species-by-species basis,
to a more comprehensive set of ecosystem-protection
laws.

An issue which is seen to be more and more urgent is
the extinction of species—whether humanity has the
right to cause or encourage the extinction of species.
There is now a new scientific discipline precisely in this
area, conservation biology. Its goal is the continuance of
biological diversity, and the major effort of many is now
to conserve entire ecosystems and to reverse and rehabili-
tate when ecosystems have been damaged.[12]

An extraordinary new technology is being created for
genetic engineering and with it many new ethical questions. Patented, genetically improved animals are now a
royalty-paying fact of life. A cloning technique for animals already exists and is now being applied to cows.

The U. S. Patent and Trademark Office has been
granting these patents but has held back from allowing
royalties in the case of human life: "The grant of a
limited but exclusive property right in a human being,"
the office explained, "is prohibited by the Constitu-

tion."[13] In legal theory with long roots in Western civilization, something a person possesses can be disposed of in three possible ways: sale as personal property, disposal as surplus, or by gift or donation. An organ of the body, according to this tradition, can be given or donated only because the human body has been regarded not as something one owns or disposes of, but as who one is—it has a mystical, spiritual quality.

The new environmental questions are not money-soluble but will require the application of our collective wisdom. Like the old conservation and environmental issues, however, greed and exploitation are always going to be in the background as human control over all phases of life on this planet advances at its relentless pace. "Leopold's manifesto was written in 1948," Ehrlich observes: "Unfortunately, the prevailing attitudes toward nature that he deplored—that natural things are valueless except as something people can exploit—are still predominant in Western culture."[14]

Leopold saw the need for people to make an "internal change," a change in loyalties, affections, and convictions if conservation is ever to move from a special cause to a popular conviction. He also saw that education, simply more education, would not bring about such internal changes. He perceived that modern life takes us *away* from the land, rather than *toward* it; this for him was the most serious obstacle impeding the evolution of a land ethic.

What Leopold failed to see, however, were the social implications of the Judaeo-Christian religious tradition. The "Mosaic Decalogue," as he called it, pertained for him only to the first level of ethical reflection, that which has to do with individual behavior. He knew that "enlightened self-interest" was not enough and grasped the limitations of government ownership as a solution. Leopold's land ethic, right in its aspiration, was skimpy in its religious and philosophical grounding. "It is tragically revealing," Peter Borelli comments, "that after one hundred years of conservation activity, 'public' is equated with 'protected,' whereas 'private' usually means 'plundered.'"[15]

2 HOME OR HOTEL: AN ETHIC FOR THE EARTH

One of the most telling aspects of our newly enlarged conception of space and time is not only the loss of a need for God as a hypothesis to explain reality but also the reduction of the significance of our planetary life. Science, laudably, enters the picture in our public discernment of moral norms, closing the gap out of necessity between the two cultures, the scientific and the humanistic. But how adequate is science taken by itself or even philosophy apart from religion as a basis for ethical discourse? That is the concern of this chapter. Scientific and technological analyses routinely enter into environmental-impact studies as necessary factors. But there are other factors as well that must be weighed.

Edward O. Wilson, the sociobiologist and self-described scientific materialist, seeks to find his ethics in biology more deeply studied. The myths of traditional religions have fatally deteriorated and the results have been dire: "a loss of moral consensus, a greater sense of helplessness about the human condition and a shrinking of concern back toward the self and the immediate future."[1] God, having lost his place in the cosmos, has retreated, if he can be found anywhere at all, according to Wilson, to the ultimate units of matter, quarks, and electron shells. This last assertion was familiar even at the time of Teilhard de Chardin and was what prompted him to elaborate a Christology in terms of cosmic evolution. The ultimate norm of morality for Wilson is to keep human genetic material intact: "Morality has no other demonstrable ultimate function."[2] Besides the survival of the genes, a biologically derived ethic would find place for the nobility of the human species and universal human rights because of our place among other mammals. The human soul, if there is one, is to be found "deep within the brain."[3]

Since humankind has evolved by Darwinian natural selection, genetic chance, and environmental necessity, we are presented at this moment of history, according to Wilson, with two great "spiritual dilemmas": The species lacks any goal external to its own biological nature—we have no particular place to go; and, secondly, in the absence of any transcendental goals, how, ethically, are we to decide, now that we can, which biological censors and motivators are to be enhanced and which ones curtailed, as we get off "automatic pilot" in our control of evolution? The only solution is to integrate the findings of the natural sciences with the social sciences and the humanities.

It is a curious exercise to read Wilson's book, which seems to have been written in a time warp. It is as if we had not lived through the post-Enlightenment, post-Darwinian period and were still in the thrall of the excitement of the new knowledge and had not experienced at all its fundamental limitations in providing precisely what Wilson is asking it to supply, namely a wisdom for life. Anyone who would claim like Wilson that he can offer a biological "explanation" of art can be expected to locate the soul in the brain and God in quarks.

Theology cannot survive as an intellectual discipline, Wilson maintains; its pleasures are mostly emotional, but "religion itself will endure for a long time. . . . Like the mythical giant Antaeus who drew energy from his mother, the earth, religion cannot be defeated by those who merely cast it down."[4] Wilson's intuition here is correct. Religion's strength is in its ties to the earth: the earth's origins, meaning, destiny beyond mere survival.

It is the conviction of this chapter that only in conjunction with a religious view of life will we be able to articulate an ethic for the earth which will not have the functional and minimalistic qualities of a hotel-like existence but the feel of a home. To begin, we must bring into focus the mutual relationships and corresponding truth-values of religion, philosophy, and science.

RELIGION, PHILOSOPHY, SCIENCE

In the medieval synthesis of all areas of knowledge, a hierarchical mode of thinking prevailed according to which theology was at the apex because of the sublimity of its subject matter, namely God, and the certainty of its truth. Theology's "handmaid" was philosophy, providing theology with a conceptual framework as well as many of the questions arising out of human experience that demanded a theological answer. At the bottom of the hierarchy was natural science because it yielded a "weaker" knowledge of God and the world. Since the Enlightenment this hierarchy has been turned upside down, with science providing the sole "objective" norm of truth. Philosophy has receded in importance as well as theology; novels and history, and in our own day, "self-help" books, have become the sources to be looked to for wisdom about life and norms of behavior.

But theology, even at the height of its influence, never sought to usurp the role of reason. Divine revelation did not relieve human intelligence of its proper investigations, although revelation could exercise what was called a "negative norm" by correcting notions considered inimical to divinely revealed truth. For example, the preexistence of the soul as found in Platonism and the eternity and necessity of creation in Aristotelianism were ruled out even though it was not considered inappropriate to use concepts from both these philosophies to explain the data of divinely revealed truth.[5]

Theology, on its part, could contribute positively to philosophy, and one of its greatest contributions was the seminal idea of "person." Since Christ is accurately described according to orthodox faith as one person in possession of two natures—one human, the other divine—then, philosophically, person and nature cannot be the same. A person "has" a nature and is not identified with nature. This philosophical breakthrough led to numerous insights about human freedom and transcendence throughout the history of philosophical thought down to our own day.

Christian philosophers have also been quick to admit that although as Christians they are bound to respect the distinctive autonomies of faith and reason, their philosophical thought might have taken them in very different directions were they not professed Christians. Etienne Gilson put it well: "It is hard for me to understand how a

Christian can ever philosophize as if he were not a Christian. The creed I learned in catechism holds all the key positions that have dominated since I was a child my interpretation of the world. The philosophy I have today is totally encompassed by religious belief."[6]

Divine revelation, although it is normative, does not disclose all of reality; there is much for philosophy, science, and the arts to explore. The problem comes when scientific findings seem to contradict some basic truth found in divine revelation. To this problem, three approaches have been made. Liberal theologians within Protestantism and "modernist" theologians in Catholicism have insisted that scientific truth must prevail and have denied or limited any special authority to the Bible or the church in the realm of truth. Neoorthodox Protestants resolve the problem by asserting there is absolutely nothing in common between scientific findings and divine revelation—they are simply different realms of knowledge. There can be no natural knowledge of God apart from revelation, and revelation has no content in terms of adding to our store of ordinary knowledge.

A traditional Catholic interpretation of the relationship of religion and science would contain these elements:

1. A natural theology apart from divine revelation can yield some knowledge of God. Psalm 104 and Romans 1:20 are classic biblical references to the reflected glory of God discoverable by all, whether professed believer or not, in the world as it exists.

2. Nature has its own integrity and rationality apart from God and science is free to follow its own principles in discovering its structures and operations.

Religious faith must never be based upon the shaky

foundation that it alone can supply information regarding matters currently lacking scientific explanation, as if God abided in the gaps of human knowledge. This "God of the gaps" received its greatest blow with the publication in 1859 by Charles Darwin of his *Origin of Species*, which offered a plausible theory as to how individual species may have originated apart from immediate creation of each by God.

3. Revelation concerns the mysteries of God, mysteries that are beyond reason to discover. These mysteries, which basically concern God's unfailing love of his creatures, a love made manifest in Jesus Christ,[7] do provide truths about ordinary life and its meaning—but these truths can never contradict truths discoverable by human reason alone, for God is the source and the ground of all truth. Faith and reason can and do interact, discovering mutual correspondences.[8]

It would be more than an oversimplification to say that "sciences deal with the world and theology with God,"[9] it would be in some ways positively misleading. It is also at least incomplete to assert, as is often done in a scientific age, that God is not a cause of events in the natural order in the sense of miraculously "intervening" from time to time. It is understandable that in the defense of religion some have sought these refuges, but they lead to a rather anemic conception of the relation of God and the world which we must avoid even, or I would say, *especially*, in a scientific age. Theology deals with God (by definition, it is "the science of God"), but any adequate understanding of God must include the world, as the process theologians continue to point out, with much basis in scripture and tradition. The world has its own autonomy, its "secularity," but it also mirrors the God who made it, however obscurely. In the biblical world-view, furthermore, the world once created does not continue on its own; it depends upon God for every moment of its continued existence. God's ever-active presence in the world is not based upon some outside and occasional "intervention" interrupting the so-called "laws" of nature, but is vastly more profound and extensive. For the religious person, the rising and setting of the sun are daily miracles.

4. St. Augustine has provided some classic formulas for the mutual competencies of faith and reason. Faith for Augustine of course is the primordial orientation for all of life and as such it precedes the operations of reason and guides them. But, he goes on, in some circumstances reason precedes faith in the sense that intelligent human beings must use their God-given intelligence to seek out rational explanations, to the extent that such is possible, even for what is believed on faith, in order that we may believe them even more.[10] Augustine also taught that God has been revealed in "two books," not one—the book of scripture and the book of nature. If there appears to be a conflict between the two, we have misinterpreted one or the other.[11]

In light of these broad principles that are characteristic of the Christian tradition, opposition by the church to Copernicus in 1543 and to Galileo in 1610 may be seen not as normative but as having their own special causes, among which are the defensiveness that descended upon the church in the post-Reformation period and extraneous political circumstances. Sometimes a hidden ideology was at work in the "warfare" between science and religion. One such ideology, it now appears in retrospect, was at work in the alliance of the Newtonian philosophy of nature as a self-operative machine with liberal Protestantism in the seventeenth century, an alliance favored by the ruling class in England, not because it offered the most plausible explanation of nature, but because it provided an underpinning of existing social arrangements.[12]

Even with these traditional principles widely known, it is still possible to have fundamental misunderstandings arise between the scientific and religious communities, often with the best of good will on both sides. For example, the noted British scientist-mathematician Stephen W. Hawking has written a helpful and searching book about the origin and fate of the universe called *A Brief History of Time: From the Big Bang to Black Holes*. As Carl Sagan writes in his introduction, the word "God" fills these pages. If it becomes possible to combine quantum mechanics with general relativity, as it seems it might, then would all be "explained"—galaxies, stars, even human beings? With the discovery of a "complete" theory, would we have, as Hawking claims, "the ultimate triumph of human reason—for then we would know the mind of God"?[13]

Hawking became interested in these cosmological questions, he reports, when he was invited to attend a conference organized at the Vatican. At that conference the pope said, according to Hawking, "that it was all right to study the evolution of the universe after the big bang, but we should not inquire into the big bang itself because that was the moment of creation and therefore the work of God. I was glad then that he did not know the subject of the talk I had just given at the conference—the possibility that space-time was finite but had no boundary, which means that it had no beginning, no moment of creation."[14] In a universe with no edges, no beginning, and no end, what was there left for the Creator to do?

What Pope John Paul II said and what Hawking heard were quite different. The pope spoke about two distinct orders of knowledge, faith and reason. He actually welcomed the search for a fundamental law, "the simplest possible, but because of its very simplicity the most difficult to grasp," to explain the universe.[15] The "big bang" and creation belong to different orders; they are as different as "how" is from "why." Creation is a theological doctrine, not a scientific theory. Even a universe of "no edges," of "no beginning and no end," would be one that came into being and is sustained in being by the creative love of God who brought order out of chaos, an order for science to explore ever more deeply. One wonders too, as Jeremy Bernstein has commented, whether Hawking's desire to construct a Theory of Everything really takes him beyond science. "In science," Bernstein writes, "one counts oneself fortunate if one succeeds in constructing a theory of something."[16]

Karl Rahner, in an article published in English after his death, insists that God cannot be considered as just another factor among many to be observed within a series of individual phenomena that the scientist works with. God is nothing less that the one and absolute ground of all realities. Creation refers to the continuing relationship of the world to its transcendent ground; it is the conviction that everything that exists must have an ultimate unity and community. Rahner actually mentions the scientific theory of the "big bang" and the attempt to place it in time, but distinguishes this theory from the truths being expressed in the doctrine of creation. When religious faith denies that time is eternal or that the universe is eternal, it is saying that everything that exists, including time itself, even if they could be said to have always existed, actually owe their existence to God, the source of all being.[17]

To commemorate the three hundredth anniversary of Newton's *Philosophiae naturalis principia mathematica*, the Holy See, in September 1987, sponsored a study week on the relationships of theology, philosophy, and the natural sciences. In his introduction to the published papers, Pope John Paul stated that a position of mere neutrality between science and religion is insufficient, even if they respect each other's competencies and limitations. "So much of our world seems to be in fragments," the pope declared, with truth and values often going their separate ways while people seek and need intellectual coherence. A new interchange could result in a vision for the world that includes "a deep reverence for all that is, a hope and assurance that the fragile goodness, beauty and life we see in the universe is moving toward a completion and fulfillment which will not be overwhelmed by the forces of dissolution and death. This vision also provides a strong support for the values which are emerging both from our knowledge and appreciation of creation and of ourselves as the products, knowers and stewards of creation."[18]

Then, making specific reference to the religious vision of the world contained in the Book of Genesis, the pope draws an illuminating parallel between the way in which Genesis itself re-interpreted the ancient stories it drew upon in its telling of the creation and the possibility of scientific advance broadening and deepening even our religious understanding of the universe. He asks:

If the cosmologies of the ancient Near Eastern world could be purified and assimilated into the first chapters of *Genesis*, might contemporary cosmology have something to offer to our reflections upon creation? Does an evolutionary perspective bring any light to bear upon theological anthropology, the meaning of the human person as the *imago Dei* (image of God), the problem of Christology and even upon the development of doctrine itself? What, if any, are the eschatological implications of contemporary cosmology, especially in light of the vast future of the universe? Can theological method fruitfully appropriate insights from scientific methodology and the philosophy of science?[19]

The pope concludes, "Science can purify religion from error and superstition; religion can purify science from idolatry and false absolutes."[20]

THE RELEVANCE OF THE BIBLE AS A SOURCE FOR ETHICS

The value and the contribution of biblical revelation for an ethic for the earth are the very qualities that caused the cultured Christians of the patristic period to "spiritualize" its meaning, and that is its irremedial connectedness to a particular place and a particular people. The embarrassment of the particular continues, of course, and Bertrand Russell invoked it in his deliberately provocative *Why I Am Not a Christian*, for to be a Christian would have required Russell to believe, as he put it, that in one particular person of one particular nation on one particular planet of one particular solar system in a potentially infinite universe, the Son of God became incarnate.

A contemporary reaction to the spiritualizing tendency within Christianity has been "creation theology" in its various forms. In the interests of a more "holistic," earth-centered view of life, some expressions of this theology have not only cancelled out the need for the redemption of the planet but also rolled back the clock by discarding distinctions that are hard-won cultural, not to say dogmatic, achievements, such as the real distinction between body, mind, and soul, and between God and his creation. For some creation theologians, too, like the "geologian" Thomas Berry, "we are in trouble right now because we do not have a good story." The old story, according to Berry, of how the world came to be is no longer adequate. "It is a sectarian story."[21]

Michael Walzer, in his provocatively everyday conception of moral philosophy and social criticism is, I believe, closer to the mark. We need not discover or invent a new story according to which we may interpret our lives. We can start from where we presently are for where we are "is always *someplace of value*, else we would never have settled there. . . . We do not have to discover the moral world because we have always lived there. We do not have to invent it because it has already been invented. . . . [T]he moral world has a lived-in quality, like a home occupied by a single family over many generations."[22]

A significant part of the moral universe of every person living within the influence of Western civilization is the Bible. Northrop Frye, following on William Blake, calls the Bible Western civilization's "great code." "Blake's line 'O Earth, O Earth return,' for example," Frye writes, "though it contains only five words and only three different words, contains also about seven direct allusions to the Bible."[23] The Bible begins where time begins, with the creation of the world; it ends where time ends, with the Book of Revelation.

"[We humans] live," Frye continues, "not directly or nakedly in nature like the animals, but within a mythological universe, a body of assumptions and beliefs developed from our existential concern. . . . Practically all that we can see of this body of concern is socially conditioned and culturally inherited. . . . The Bible is clearly a major element in our own imaginative tradition, whatever we may think we believe about it."[24]

According to another literary critic, Harold Bloom, "Biblical men and women tend to resemble Shakespeare's characters and Freud's descriptions of the psyche precisely because the Bible . . . has invented our literary sense of human personality, and so has bequeathed to Shakespeare and to Freud alike what remains our universal sense of human experience. . . . If the Bible is unique . . . it is because we remain enclosed by it, whether we overtly believe in it or not," he continues. "How do you criticize the structures that set most of the terms for order that allow you to read coherently, or teach you to approach experience in the light of literature?"[25]

These literary approaches contain many riches in their reading of the Bible, riches that elude the excavatory forays of those exegetes trained exclusively in the historical-critical method. But a literary appreciation of the Bible, however enlightening, necessarily falls short in its understanding of a book—or, more properly, of a library of books—that on its own terms is intended to be the record of God's revelation. "*Revelare*," the Latin root of the word "revelation," means "to uncover." God's revelation "uncovers" the previously hidden mystery that has always lain at the heart of existence. Revelation claims to be the "truth" of that existence. Blake himself pointed to the difference between a scientific and a religious grasp of ultimate reality when he described the contrasting reactions to a sunrise by a scientist and by himself as a religious person: One sees only a thin wafer of light coming from a distant star, but what Blake sees is a vision of the fiery cherubim and seraphim ecstatically praising God! The Bible claims to offer such deeper truths that, if they be truths at all, will be vindicated over and over again in the experience of all persons whether they believe in its revelation or not. This is the moral universe Walzer is talking about, the world we inhabit rather than discover or invent. "Like the physical world, like life itself," he writes, "morality is a creation; but we are not its creators. God makes it, and we come, with his help and with the help of his servants, to know about it and then to admire it and study it."[26]

Walzer contrasts the sharp critical edge and moral bite of a divinely revealed morality—Do this! Don't do that!—with the morality of secular discovery and invention. Those who seek to discover moral principles apart from God establish their objectivity by adopting "no particular point of view" and by a process of stepping back to examine life from a critical distance. "I doubt that we can ever step back all the way to nowhere," Walzer comments. "Even when we look at the world from *somewhere else*, however, we are still looking at the world. We are looking, in fact, at a particular world; we may see it with special clarity, but we will not discover anything that isn't already there. Since the particular world is also our own world, we will not discover anything that isn't already here. Perhaps this is a general truth about secular (moral) discoveries; if so, it suggests what we lose when we lose our belief in God."[27]

Those others who purport not so much to discover morality as to invent one, "create what God would have created if there were a God,"[28] namely, a universal corrective for all the differing social codes by which people live. To respond to the philosophical and scientific inventors of morality, Walzer summons the image of a transcultural group of travelers converging somewhere in outer space. There they work out a universal, if minimal, morality among themselves. In other words, they design an ideal hotel room, an anonymous space with the minimum requirements for living and with many useful conveniences. But what these space travelers "commonly *want*, however, is not to be permanently registered in a hotel but to be established in a new home, a dense moral culture, within which they can feel some sense of belonging."[29]

Walzer argues for a social morality that is the work of priests and prophets, teachers and sages, storytellers, poets, historians, and writers generally, all arguing among themselves in an endless task of interpretation. They stand a little to the side of their societies, but not outside; they are friends, not enemies; they want things to go well; "critical distance is measured in inches."[30] He contrasts the prophecies of the biblical Jonah, who carried a thin, general call to repentance to a foreign people, and of Amos who has particular charges to make against his own people, a people united by a conviction of divine election and convenant. Amos's prophesy makes no sense apart from Jewish law, but within that law he picks and chooses to make his own pointed reinterpretation.

Ethical systems are being constructed to help us live responsibly and happily on our planet, but they often strike us as deficient for the reasons Walzer alleges: they tell us what we already know, or they project a hotel-type existence as their model, or they fail to evoke anything in us that would inspire dedication or personal sacrifice. Love my neighbor as myself: Why should I love anyone *that much*? Why should I care, whatever the statistics say about ozone levels, rain forests, endangered species?

An ethic that employs the Bible as our most available story would of necessity have to heighten elements of the story that perhaps have not been so emphasized before, the "picking and choosing" that are always part of prophecy. But this is not to falsify the biblical message, to make it say something other than what it means to say. It is rather to do what every prophet must do when, in looking at the sins of an age, he/she points to "the one thing necessary." Such an ethic, though biblically inspired, would have to draw upon as well all that philosophy and science have to offer in applying its wisdom to concrete decisions and actions.

THE VALUE AND LIMITS OF PHILOSOPHY AND SCIENCE IN ETHICS

There is a major discussion that is vigorously being pursued in contemporary ethics concerning the specificity of Christian ethics. No one would argue that the church invented morality—morality pertains to the given structures of life. In this sense ethics has its own rationality and autonomy apart from religion. Philosophy and science are to be consulted among other areas of human knowledge and experience to provide an adequate basis for moral teaching. There is no substitute for the use of human reason in moral matters, even in a religious context.

Going further, some Christian ethicists have argued that the Christian faith can "only" supply to ethics a new Christian meaning, motivation, and insight: It is up to Christians themselves to decide which innerworldly behavior is consistent with their faith. There is no escaping such responsibility by appealing to natural goals imbedded in nature or to God's ordinances and commands. The "naturalistic fallacy" makes the illegitimate leap from natural functions to moral instructions, and the appeal to divine commands seems to place the transcendent God alongside the objects of his creation.

Thus Josef Fuchs concludes his essay, "Christian Morality: Biblical Orientations and Human Evaluation," with this paragraph:

> Correct human behavior in this human world is to be discovered by the partner created by the Creator, and with the aid of the human reason of the creature which reflects the wisdom of the Creator. Biblical faith necessitates this process and gives its own orientation as a help toward fulfiling it, without however substituting itself for human reason. Enlightened human reason itself must seek the moral rightness of inner-worldly behavior (and truly evaluate it), thus concretizing the biblical orientation in a manner which is independent of it.[31]

While this debate is going on among Christian ethicists, a different kind of discussion is taking place among moral philosophers with no particular religious allegiance, and it concerns the limits of human reason in establishing moral norms. Bernard Williams in his *Ethics and the Limits of Philosophy* concludes that "the demands of the modern world on ethical thought are unprecedented, and the ideas of rationality embodied in most contemporary moral philosophy cannot meet them."[32] To Socrates' question about how one should live, philosophy today has given up hope that it can provide a reasonable answer. Ethics is what the ancients called *disposition* and *custom* and their multifaceted reality, Williams argues, cannot be reduced to certain fundamental ethical principles. A rationalistic conception of morality requires "in principle every decision to be based on grounds that can be discursively explained,"[33] and this is clearly impossible.

Some have sought hope, after the departure of religion, in a community of reason, but as Williams notes, such a dream is too far removed from social and historical reality "and from any concrete sense of a particular ethical life."[34] Philosophy and science have their contribution to make to what Williams calls "reflective living," but he adds, "to suppose that if their formulations are rejected we are left with *nothing* is to take a strange view of what in social and personal life counts for something."[35]

Fuchs, we may say, is far too modest in his claims for a biblically based morality. He wishes to avoid a fundamentalistic understanding of the sacred writings by trying to make them solve problems that were never conceived of at the time of their origins; to try to find in the "relatively few statements in the Bible itself" moral norms for decisions in the immense field of contemporary life is, according to him, "a hopeless project." "In particular," he adds, "this way of proceeding contradicts the whole tendency of the Bible, above all of the New Testament, not to offer itself primarily as a help for the right ordering of the human world, but as a help for salvation, and therefore, for conversion and for personal goodness, now that the kingdom of God has broken into the world."[36] Leaving aside this last, highly debatable contention, Fuchs seems to assume as almost inconsequential the essential ingredient in the formation of moral thinking and acting that Williams and others has pointed out as missing in nonreligious ethical systems—the very conceptual and motivational context for social and personal life that religion traditionally has supplied.

In taking note, as Fuchs does, of the contribution of biblical faith to the process of formulating moral norms and judgments, he acknowledges that such a faith helps us to have a different and even unique conception of ourselves as persons which yields an ethic that is not just *autonomous* but *theonomous,* that is, based upon a vision of God especially as God has been revealed to us by Christ. And this, I am sure Fuchs would quickly affirm, is no small contribution indeed.

Walzer is correct when he says that what matters is not so much the biblical text but the interpretation of the text: Judaism, for him, is all about interpretation. Moral wisdom is the by-product of the learned rabbis endlessly arguing among themselves—and *that's all there is.* From a Christian, and especially from a Catholic perspective, there is something more. There are certain criteria for the legitimacy of any interpretation of the biblical story.

Certainly the apostolic witness of the church in her formative period is one. The patristic exegesis of the Bible is another. So also is the living in the truth of revelation by the church of all ages as manifested by the authoritative teachings of her popes and bishops. This continued living in the truth of revelation cannot alter what was originally given but can show its relevance to questions that were never conceived before but which are still within the scope of its holy wisdom to enlighten.

In her essay on Yiddish literature, Cynthia Ozick describes the biblical world inhabited by those who developed this tongue as their vernacular. "In its tenderer mien," she writes, "Yiddish is capable of a touching conversational intimacy with a consoling and accessible God. If Yiddish lacks cathedral grandeur, there is a compensation of coziness, of smallness, of a lovingly close, emphatic, and embracing Creator, who can be appealed to in the diminutive. Yiddish is a household tongue, and God, like other members of the family, is sweetly informal in it."[37] God and his Mother and saints are likewise described by James Joyce as "members of the family" for Irish Catholics. No educated person in this scientific age would ever be tempted to place God, in the phrase of Fuchs, "alongside the objects of his creation" and still find him believable. But neither would genuinely religious persons fail to achieve sufficient familiarity and intimacy with the transcendent Creator so as to discern to some extent his will for them in the world and, occasionally, with ample biblical precedent, to question him about his purposes in making us at all. It is precisely out of such intimations of God's will and our continuing arguments with him that the world becomes our home, a moral universe.

But the vision of God given us by Christ is not merely that of the Creator: it is of the God who loves the world so much that he sends his only Son. The coming of the Son signals the end of the present era and sounds an urgent eschatological note for human behavior; we are to "repent" *for* the "kingdom of God is at hand."[38] We are to love both friend and enemy because of God's own boundless love manifested in Christ. Christian ethics, then, goes beyond an ethics of reason discoverable in creation and is fundamentally shaped and formed by the values of the coming kingdom. This moral vision provides not merely models of conduct and a new ethical perspective but also prescribes very specific ways of acting in this present world in order to be consistent with the values of the kingdom. What is called "natural" is inserted into a Christian context, one that calls for a better and higher justice.

This is what is new about Christian ethics, and what makes it such a powerful motivating force for hope and human action. It is a clear alternative to a "dualism based on a godless world and a worldless god."[39]

3 THE SILENCE OF SPACE, THE ETERNITY OF TIME

The publication in 1859 of Darwin's *Origin of Species* changed unalterably the human appreciation of nature. Because nature and God are so closely aligned, a change in our conception of the material universe brings about the viable reappraisal of our ideas about God. Like the Copernican revolution centuries before, the theory of evolution also changed the human understanding of God. These effects are pictorially evident as we consider, for example, the way nature was portrayed by the Hudson River school at a time when Darwinism's impact had not yet been felt, and how totally old-fashioned such paintings now appear to our modern sensibility.

The Hudson River school spans most of the decades of the nineteenth century and encompasses three distinct generations of painters. These artists found in the nearby wilderness an American paradise. Though naturalistic in style, the paintings reveal a natural world redolent of the optimism, the elevated moral tone, and the concept of beauty of their creators. The scale of these paintings communicates the awesomeness of the natural scenes which are rendered with theatrical interplays of light and darkness, cascading streams, and sharply falling cliffs seen from dramatic angles of vision. A final phase of the Hudson River school presented scenes of profound stillness and luminosity that embued them with a meditative aura.

As the century drew to its close, the work of Thomas Cole, founder of the school, and of his successors seemed very out of date. The country was changing in the direction of urbanization and industrialization. But even more subtly views of nature had changed thanks to Darwin; nature was no longer the paradise of God but the object of scientific research.[1] Thus reimaged, nature did not reflect back reassuring messages about the centrality of human values and concerns but told a different story of a random and long historical process with human presence not center stage but at the fringes of an unfathomable universe.

Religious reactions to the new vistas opened up by scientific speculations have not been lacking. We cite below a few significant ones within Christianity, both Catholic and Protestant.

On the Catholic side, Blaise Pascal may be given as an early example of one who decided in the interests of faith simply to live in two worlds without attempting to bring them into harmony. A later Catholic scientist, on the other hand, and one very much conscious of Pascal's dilemma, Pierre Teilhard de Chardin sought to bring about a grand synthesis in which human and religious history as well as the entire universe are all organically integrated into one single growth and one single process and progress. Pascal's mysticism, while keeping the two cultures, religious and scientific, separate, did have the advantage of preserving those aspects of each which are truly incommensurate with the other. Teilhard's synthesizing attempts, on the other hand, brought the two into often illuminating contact, but merit the criticism of not respecting adequately the different levels and methodologies being employed.

On the Protestant side, I mention the name of Joseph Sittler who in our time is associated with the need for a more environmentally adequate theology. Sittler, like many Protestant theologians, does not look with sympathy upon Teilhard whose work seems tinged with an apologetic concern to make Roman Catholicism a necessary part of the cosmic evolution. Jürgen Moltmann and John Cobb, both more systematic theologians than Sittler, have employed insights from science to elaborate new conceptions of God and God's relationship to the universe, usually along the lines of process philosophy. They may be cited as two significant attempts across the Reformation divide to bring theology into the new scientific age.

CATHOLIC APPROACHES

Two hundred years before Darwin the philosopher-mathematician Blaise Pascal (1623–62), in the aftermath of the Copernican revolution, found himself frightened by the eery stillness and emptiness of infinite space. He wrote in one of his philosophical fragments: "When I consider the short duration of my life, absorbed in the eternity preceding and following it, the little space which I fill, and even that I see, engulfed in the infinite immensity of spaces which I do not know and which do not know me, I am frightened. . . ."[2] Pascal was a fervent, believing Christian and solved his dilemma by choosing not to think about Copernicus and the meaning of his discoveries; he chose instead to believe even more ardently in God, and not just God but the "God of Jesus Christ, the God of Abraham, the God of Isaac, the God of Jacob, not of the philosophers and savants."[3] He chose to believe in God who is not the deistic God of a machine-like universe that once made spins on its own, but God who is a localized God, a personal God who revealed himself to particular persons in a particular place. He chose to believe in this very specific God, God who is "my Father," not so much with his mind as with his heart, for, as he wrote in a justly famous formula, "It is the heart that knows God, not the reason . . . The heart has its reasons that reason knows nothing of."[4]

A fellow countryman of Pascal from the same region of France was to take up Pascal's apologetic for Christianity at a later moment in history and strive to move it forward along similar mystical lines in confronting a new challenge, in his case the challenge of Darwin: the Jesuit paleontologist Pierre Teilhard de Chardin[5] (1881–1955) who shared in the discovery of the "Peking Man."

Teilhard's major theological work, *Le milieu divin* was written under an impulse very similar to that which prompted Pascal to write. The universe, according to Teilhard, appears inevitably to anyone who is "neither simpleton nor child" to be a "vast horrible thing," "this grim enormity," a "menacing reality" and "universal horror."[6] Only by faith in the Gospels could one discern in it the adorable presence of a divine goodness.

Teilhard's principal concern was a plainer disclosing of God in a world existing, as he learned from Copernicus and Galileo, in an immensity of space, and as

Darwin discovered, in an immensity of time. Teilhard wished to create a theological vocabulary large enough to encompass these discoveries. Evolution became "Christogenesis," the whole universe undergoing a great metamorphosis as part of the universal resurrection brought about by the cosmic Christ.

In his attempt to give new credibility to Christianity in a scientific age, Teilhard strove to overthrow the scientific prejudice that the meaning of things is to be found by getting down to their smallest elements; on the contrary, he proposed, a coherent picture of the world as it continues to evolve must flow from what he called a "Christic," that is, from a personal and transcendent center. Neither did he accede to the scientific pretension that the true and objective are only those things susceptible to scientific analysis; for this scientific mysticism he substituted another mysticism not unlike "the reasons of the heart" that Pascal found so compelling.

Teilard's abiding significance lies in his fervent desire to reconcile "the two halves of our lives," the seemingly contradictory principles coexisting in his own life, in contemporary culture, and in the spirituality of French Catholicism.[7] In his own words, he wished to overcome the dichotomies and dualisms of God and the world, humanity and Christianity, religious detachment and worldly activity, creation and redemption, the natural and the supernatural, the soul and the earth, spirit and matter, himself as priest and scientist. He wished to unite them all into one love, one universe, one divine milieu—into God who is at once the center and the environment for everything that exists. A descendant both of religious believers and of Voltaire, Teilhard espoused a "vigorous naturalism" within which Christ was immersed. To be a

Christian need not mean to be less a human, less a scientist, but rather more so. Everywhere he sought "affinities," "sympathies" between the two realms. "I find it difficult to express what a sense of fulfillment, ease, and of being at home I find in this world of electrons, nuclei and waves," he wrote.[8] A few days before his death on an Easter Sunday, Teilhard wrote his own Pascalian *Mémorial* under the title "What I Believe." In a few scraps of sentences he recapitualed his lifework in the Pauline verse about the final result of Christ's resurrection, namely "that God may be all in all."[9] The organicity of everything in the universe was for Teilhard a primordial scientific and religious truth and the basis of any ethic of modern life. Like others who came after, Teilhard showed an openness to pantheism, not in any crude sense of merging God with what God has made, but as an expression, however inexact, of the organicity of all that exists. "The pantheist tendency," he wrote, "is so universal and so persistent that it must have in it a soul of naturally Christian truth that we must baptize."[10]

Teilhard's major works, *Le milieu divin* and *Le phenomène humain*, were published only after his death because of the religious difficulties of his ideas. In his introduction to *Le phenomène humain*, Sir Julian Huxley wrote with exactness that Teilhard saw everything *sub specie evolutionis*, that is, with "reference to its development in time and to its evolutionary position."[11] *Sub specie evolutionis*, however, is not the same as seeing everything *sub specie aeternitatis*. Even his sympathetic defender Henri De Lubac had to concede that Teilhard seemed "unduly influenced by a too empirical and too purely temporal picture of the things of the spirit."[12] To make Christ the Alpha and the Omega of the universe,

Teilhard sought to make this Christ or, as he called him, this "Super-Christ," coextensive with the physical immensities of duration and space. But the risen Christ, according to St. Paul in the same passage from First Corinthians that was so central to Teilhard's thought and speculation, is not natural or earthly but heavenly and spiritual.[13] Teilhard here becomes too much the phenomenologist.

Inflating the traditional theological vocabulary with esoteric neologisms to fit the evolutionary mode, as Teilhard tended to do, in the end must be said not to have been particularly helpful. "Super-Christ" is not really an improvement upon the New Testament; in fact, it tends to obscure its particularist point that God was incarnated in Jesus of Nazareth.

There is also part of the Teilhardian world-view a Bergsonian, quasi-Platonist conception of matter as mirage and illusion and as having no place in the heavenly consummation. His commentator De Lubac claims he helped in this respect to sweep away "the mirage of all the 'Judaic fables' and all the paradises of Mahomet."[14] While it is notoriously difficult to maintain one's balance in handling the things of heaven and of earth, the materiality of the "Judaic fables" about eternity may be less misleading than hyped-up images of a Christ somehow working himself out in an evolutionary process.

The contemporary poet A. R. Ammons has been praised for his "post-Christian" veracity and integrity in describing human life as a frail butterfly, "a lightly guided piece of trash the wind takes ten thousand miles."[15] Rejecting the special creation of human life as incompatible with the "fact" of evolution, Ammons's poems are said to suggest a "many-sided view of reality" and the "adoption of tentative, provisional latitudes, replacing the partial, unified, prejudicial and the rigid." Ammons advocates rather "an ethics founded on the possibility of cultural illumination and human concern."[16]

This is small guidance indeed for our much-afflicted planet. Does the evolutionary world-view come to this, that we are bravely to accept everything, ourselves included, as "a lightly guided piece of trash"? Of course this mentality is precisely the one Teilhard de Chardin was confronting and, for all the shortcomings of his attempt, it seems even more breathtaking in its courage and faith not only in God but in the worth of what he called "the human phenomenon." Christ served for Teilhard as the center of value, the value of personal life above all, his "reason of the heart" that the "tentative, provisional attitudes" emanating from scientism could never replicate.

The abiding legacy of Teilhard de Chardin can be detected in the Second Vatican Council and especially in its pastoral constitution *Gaudium et spes* ("On the Church in the World of Today") which manifests, some would say now in retrospect, an excess of the Teilhardian optimism about the modern world whose problems are described as part of a "crisis of growth."[17]

The council, like Teilhard, takes note of the fact that humankind is substituting a dynamic and more evolutionary concept of nature for a static one and as a result is encountering an immense series of new problems calling for a new endeavor of analysis and synthesis. Christ is declared to be "the key, center and purpose" of history, Christ who is the image of the invisible God and simultaneously "the firstborn of all creation."[18]

The ethical implications of the council's analysis of scientific advance coupled with an enlarged theological vision are, first of all, the dignity and transcendence of the human peson as a center of freedom and individual conscience that are inviolable and, secondly, the fundamentally communitarian nature of human life. The building of a society in which personal rights are respected and social justice is promoted requires, according to the council, something more than a merely "individualistic morality" but a recognition of life in solidarity with others, wherein all have the means to exercise responsibility and to participate.[19]

The principle of the "rightful autonomy of earthly affairs" is enunciated according to which "methodical research in all branches of knowledge, provided it is carried out in a truly scientific manner and does not override moral laws, can never conflict with the faith, because the things of the world and the things of faith derive from the same God."[20]

Teilhard, as he says in Le milieu divin, is doing battle with a spirituality that speaks in such terms as "God wants only souls," and which exalts detachment from worldly pursuits as its hallmark. Teilhard boldly asserted that God himself was working by extension through human creative efforts. These efforts are given more, not less, incentive by religious faith, for faith teaches, according to Teilhard, that this earthly life continues into eternity through the power of Christ's resurrection and through the results of human activity which have in them the quality of the "definitive."[21]

The Second Vatican Council is more circumspect than Teilhard about the final form of the future planned by God and the role to be played by human agency in bringing that future about. It teaches that indeed God is preparing a "new dwelling and a new earth," already foreshadowed in our present existence. But it is also careful to distinguish "earthly progress from the increase of the kingdom of Christ," and as for the results of human activity, the council says simply "we will find them again," when the kingdom arrives, "cleansed of sin, illuminated and transfigured."[22]

On the occasion of the centenary of the birth of Teilhard, the Vatican issued a statement which seems a just appraisal. It speaks of his "powerful poetic insight," his praiseworthy dialog with science, his dauntless optimism. "But," it continues, "the complexity of the problems tackled as well as the variety of approaches adopted, have not failed to raise difficulties which rightly require a critical and serene study—both on the scientific and on the philosophical and theological levels—of this exceptional work."[23]

Gaudium et spes, which bears a Teilhardian influence, itself has given rise to tendencies which have been the subject of intense debate. This pastoral constitution was the impetus for the liberation and political theologies which came into prominence in the post-conciliar period. While these theologies provided a needed corrective upon more privatized forms of Christian life and abstract presentations of the Christian faith, they have been faulted, among other things, for their onesided anthropocentrism. The great Christian symbol of the coming reign of God, to take one notable example, has sometimes been interpreted as if it referred to new social arrangements rather than in its full cosmic dimensions and as God's transcendent gift.

The process theologian John Cobb has criticized the

Catholic political theolgian Johann Baptist Metz for failing to go beyond a sociologically based theology to one with a broader, more ecological sweep.[24] Metz would deny that his theology is sociology. "The faith of Christians," in Metz's definition, "is a praxis in history and society that is to be understood as hope in solidarity in the God of Jesus as a God of the living and the dead who calls all persons to be subjects in his presence."[25] The focus of Metz's theology is history, that is, human civilization, politics, the city, urbanization, industrialization. Nature, according to Metz, as a metaphysical category, has "wrecked itself" against the problem of history. This line of thought, according to Cobb, has proven to be a disaster so far as the human relationship to the rest of the created universe is concerned. Prior moral limits to human activity are greatly undermined in this subjectivized, post-Kantian world.

PROTESTANT APPROACHES

A theology for the environment presents a special challenge for modern inheritors of the Protestant Reformation which characteristically has emphasized divine revelation over human reason in our knowledge of God, the Gospel over nature, the deeds of God in history over any natural revelation, the order of redemption over the order of creation, Christ over the Father and the Holy Spirit. The reproach of Lynn White, Jr., in his much-cited (some would say too-much cited) essay on "The Historical Roots of Ecologic Crisis," published in 1967, touched a nerve. White lays the blame for our environmental crisis at the door of the Bible itself and accuses Christianity in particular of a special arrogance toward nature. Human domination of the entire physical creation is sanctioned in the Book of Genesis, according to White, and has given an open door to the unfolding environmental tragedy we are perpetrating.[26] The Lutheran pastor Paul Santmire felt prompted to write an entire book, *The Travail of Nature: The Ambiguous Ecological Promise of Christian Theology*, in response to White.

Some Protestant theologians who have seen the need for a theology of the environment still find difficulty with any natural theology or natural law, which has traditionally been associated with Catholicism, while others of them more radically have attempted to move beyond traditional conceptions of God in the direction of process theology. Of these theologians, Joseph Sittler is commonly regarded as a pioneer of the former tendency and Jürgen Moltmann and John Cobb as prominent among the latter.

Joseph Sittler in the 1960's perceived the need to rethink the doctrine of nature and grace because of the impact of threats to the environment. The relationship needs to be freshly approached not only because of the seriousness of the environmental issues but also because of the anthropological implications of modern science and culture. The old creation/redemption/sanctification schema, according to Sittler, is too restrictive to handle a more organic conception of life and in particular of human life as unalterably part of the web of nature. Christology itself can lead the way if it is "expanded to its cosmic dimensions, made passionate by the pathos of this threatened earth and made ethical by the love and the wrath of God."[27]

Sittler in his essays looks behind the Reformation polemics to the ampler conceptions of nature and grace found in New Testament and patristic sources and also looks beyond the medieval world to more modern conceptions of God in the work of Alfred North Whitehead. In his impressionistic style Sittler caught many of the dimensions of the problem and sketched out directions for further thought.

Jürgen Moltmann's theology of a crucified and suffering God and his theology of hope have enjoyed a great vogue, in the United States especially. Allied with the political theologians, Moltmann places emphasis on the future, upon a God who is neither intraworldly nor extraworldly but the God of Hope who is always "before" us; in this way he helped to change eschatology—the doctrines about God's absolute future and definitive salvation of the universe—from an appendage to theology to its very center of concern.

As early as his book *The Crucified God*, Moltmann saw the need for a Christian liberation of modern life, a liberation that is economic, political, and cultural.[28] Moltmann has taken up the ecological theme explicitly in two later works: *Trinity and the Kingdom* (1981) and *God in Creation: A New Theology of Creation and the Spirit of God* (1985). In these books, Moltmann actually does much of the work of developing a theology of the creation and of the environment that Sittler was calling for, with a peculiar Reformation twist and with an inclination in the direction of process theology ("God *in* creation"). Like Teilhard de Chardin, Moltmann gives a unified perspective that brings together the biblical account of creation with the findings of natural science and the theory of evolution; like Teilhard, also, he runs the danger of equating the coming kingdom of God with the supposed goal of the evolutionary process.

Moltmann in his latest book goes beyond the Reformation's exclusive emphasis upon the Second Person of the divine Trinity by elaborating the more traditional doctrine of the indwelling of the Third Person, the Holy Spirit, in the creation as the "home of God." The world as it presently exists, however, is in an alienated condition and is not God's home or ours. In the "new heavens and the new earth" alone will we enter God's Sabbath rest. God's creative act at the beginning is described along the lines of the Jewish kabbalistic idea of the divine *zimzum*—God's withdrawing within himself to create an emptiness for creatures to fill. The world then inevitably is experienced as a place of "God-forsakeness," a favorite description of Moltmann of our present existence, until the final consummation when God will once again be "all in all."

Here we see the power of Moltmann's ideas which situate human life and its present tragedies within the perspective of a future hope. But, we would have to add, the position that Moltmann adopts with regard to nature in its *present* reality severely limits the value of his theology in addressing the very environmental issues he wishes to encompass. It is obvious that for him the world now in no sense can be called the house of God, that nature itself is "the reality of that world which is no longer God's creation and is not yet God's kingdom."[29] There can be no natural knowledge of God apart from divine revelation. Human beings today are not made in the "image of God." "The true likeness to God is to be found not at the beginning of God's history with humankind, but at its end."[30] In the tradition of the Reformation, Moltmann declares, "The restoration or new creation of the likeness to God comes about in the fellowship of believers with Christ: since he is the messianic *imago Dei*, believers become *imago Christi*, and through this enter upon the path which will make them *gloria Dei* on earth."[31]

One might conclude that only Christians, according to Moltmann, will enter the heavenly rest. And how can Christians without some common ground in nature and human reason enter into common discussion and action on behalf of the environment with the majority of the people of the world who are not Christian? Neither can we agree with the assessment that the earth is totally "God-forsaken." Moltmann like Metz has seen the effects of industrial capitalism and urbanization upon religious practice and upon the environment. Metz in particular has predicted that this "Europeanization" of the whole world cannot be halted and sees no hope for a religious rebirth emanating from the Third World since even there progress is identified with the same "Europeanization." In addition, Moltmann has experiences as a prisoner of war to color his assessment of the present world order and has seen how "nature" can be perverted into a mythology of race based upon blood and soil. But more positive evaluations are possible which, without denying the perversities of sin, can detect God's creating and redeeming hand in the world as it exists and which give us solid grounds for hope in the future of our planet.

Moltmann's recasting of classical theism in terms of God's involvement in human suffering has much in common with process theology, but for Alfred North Whitehead and Charles Hartshorne, the progenitors of process theology, and their contemporary exponents such as John Cobb, it is not just classical theism that comes up short but the very God of the Bible is "beyond belief" for contemporary persons.[32] For Whitehead, God is immanent in the world and the world is immanent in God. God is part of the structure of every event as its relevant possibilities and as "lures for feeling" (God's "consequent" nature). There is then for process theology no divine guarantee that there will be a blissful final outcome to the universe—it takes human freedom too seriously for that. Hartshorne teaches a "panpsychism," which holds that all life has value for itself and for God apart from human valuing and control, and that life is to be respected from the smallest cell up through to the human community. Not all things, obviously, have the same intrinsic value. Richness of experience is Cobb's criterion for the relative worth of living beings. Though human life is unique, as part of the web of life it shares with all life a right to life. Such a right is not, however, absolute: Every animal, every human life has intrinsic value and is both an end and a means.[33]

Pantheism, as we saw in the case of Teilhard, has been sympathetically regarded by those who reverence nature as a divine manifestation. Orthodox believers, nonetheless, have generally resisted the temptation to adopt what they regard as a corruption of strict theism. Here Hartshorne offers his bipolar concept of God as a more adequate expression of what is valid in both theism and pantheism, something he calls "panentheism." According to panentheism, God is both immanent in, and comprehensive of, the world of changing, individual, dependent beings, and at the same time is eternal, absolute, and transcendent.

In classical theism, creatures have relations to God but God has no real relation to his creatures. Hartshorne responds with his doctrine of "surrelativism," a higher unity and synthesis of "relativism" and "absolutism": "God", as he says, "is absolute, yet related to all."[34]

It is certainly true that some conceptions of divinity, especially of the deist variety, have so exaggerated the divine transcendence that creatures can conceivably live on their own once created. Other conceptions of God, for example the neoorthodox version of a totally transcendent, totally "Other" being, as espoused by Karl Barth, have had the paradoxical effect of reducing the world and everything in it to a secularity which could drain them of religious meaning. These exaggerations are ripe targets for correction by process theology. But God as portrayed in the scriptures could hardly fit the deist or neoorthodox description. "It is in him that we live and move and have our being,"[35] Paul declares in Acts. Far from being uninvolved in earthly affairs, God in the Bible shows, almost scandalously, the emotions of anger, jealousy, the capacity to relent and change his mind as well as to feel genuine sorrow and heartfelt mercy and love.

The involvement of God in the world reached an entirely new level in the incarnation of God's only Son who, in the memorable words of *Gaudium et spes*, "worked with human hands, thought with a human mind, acted with a human will and loved with a human heart."[36] And to the human protest arising to God regarding the suffering, injustice, and death that we experience, as Pope John Paul II has written, God does not respond in the abstract: "In fact, we cannot help noticing that the one to whom we put the question is himself suffering and answers from the cross, from out of his own suffering."[37] Classic theism certainly would have to be stretched almost to unrecognizable proportions to accommodate these facts of the Christian revelation.

Cobb, under the challenge of political theologians like Metz to influence public affairs, has written *Process Theology as Political Theology*. Unlike Metz, Cobb as a process theologian would not oppose in principle relativizing Christianity itself in his advocacy of what amounts to a new religion of life.[38] According to this religion, life is God and not the other way around. Because of its philosophical bent, process theology also shows its limitedness by lacking the capacity to convince or change humanity except by the power of rational argument. There is no place in process for a Christ who challenges the established order, reverses perspectives, and comes down on the side of the poor and the oppressed. Yet, for all these limitations, Cobb has advanced the discussion of an ethic for the new environmental challenge and has highlighted many potentialities for such an ethic within the Christian tradition itself.

THE PLACE OF NATURE

In a significant essay, Gordon Kaufman writes about nature as a "problem" for theology. Kaufman defines nature, or the natural world, as the totality of processes and powers that make up the universe, including human existence. It is something which exists independently of human artifice. He goes on to say, in Kantian terms, that "nature appears to be a nontheological, nonaxiological order within which emerges purposive and valuing activity" by humanity. The "supernatural" for Kaufman is "an unwarranted mythological redoubling of the former."[39]

"The rest of creation," in this view, apart from humanity, "is primarily material for the Creator's (and man's) purposes. . . . It has no will or purpose of its own; it knows no moral values and has no freedom of choice. It is there, thus, simply to be used by God and by man as they carry out their purposes." This is in keeping with Kant's conception that only human beings with their rational wills are ends in themselves.

If nature, furthermore, is seen as "fallen" and sin-ridden, then it is entirely opaque in relation to God. Sometimes the creation of nature itself, as in the theology of Paul Tillich, is considered a fall from grace. Thus Moltmann claims that nature "does not shine of itself but only reflects the light of future glory."[40]

These are typical Reformation views. There is no doubt that in an environmental age they constitute a "problem."

Nature in the Catholic tradition has an integrity and a finality of its own apart from grace, an integrity and a finality which, though impeded and wounded by human sinfulness, cannot in this way be destroyed. Creation is not a fall from grace nor an absence of God but a reflection, even in its fallen state, of God's power and divinity, as we read in the Letter to the Romans.[41]

The fact that God is said in the scriptures to create by a free act of his will and love does not mean that God's will is to be understood in the positivistic sense that creation is simply an arbitrary thing and makes no internal sense apart from the use God makes of it. In the scriptural view, as we will see in the next chapter, God's will in its terms is what nature means in ours.

For Cobb, what he terms "conservative" Christianity is committed to a mechanistic view of nature with an accompanying supernaturalism that separates God from the world. Such a view, Cobb maintains, has "little to do with the Bible."[42] Whatever may be the positions of the conservative Christians Cobb is citing, in traditional Catholic theology, the term "supernatural" is introduced to affirm the free gift of divine grace and intimacy which goes beyond what is "natural" and therefore "owed" to creatures as part of their intrinsic finality. But, according to this same theology, in actual history, there never was a time when the natural world was not so "elevated." As the Second Vatican Council taught, all of humanity, and not merely believers, are called to one and the same destiny, and that destiny is divine.[43]

The creation account in the Book of Genesis introduces the Pentateuch which records the gracious deeds of God as well as the persistent sinfulness of humanity. The creation story is part of the story of Israel and it stands as a prophetic judgment upon what humanity has done with God's beautiful handiwork. When Jesus was asked about Moses' allowing divorce, Jesus used Genesis as his standard and says it was not like this "from the beginning"; Moses allowed divorce only "because of the hardness of your hearts."[44] The primordial condition of creation therefore forms a norm for present behavior redeemed from sinfulness.

It is possible then for Christians to discuss rationally the right ordering of nature with nonbelievers because nature apart from grace has its own rationality. But such rational discourse does not exhaust the full meaning of nature which must be seen, from the Christian viewpoint, as both created and redeemed by God. Nature is alive with its own life and with the life of God.

4 GENESIS

When we read in church the majestic account of how "in the beginning God created the heavens and the earth" and about "the mighty wind which swept over the surface of the watery abyss"—the opening words of the Book of Genesis and of the entire Bible—it is in the liturgical context of the Easter Vigil. During the vigil, the nightwatch for the resurrection of Christ from the dead, the birthday of the world is being celebrated, as well as the beginnings of its definitive remaking in Christ. In that setting of prayer and song, the story of the creation forms the first part of a long series of readings from both Testaments that comprises the family history of the people of God.Through it we find our lives upon the planet and their brief duration situated within the long chronicle of God's dealings with his creation from its very beginning; we listen attentively to the telling of these stories once again for clues as to how we are to live in the present as well as for hints as to the meaning and purpose of all we do and experience. What we are being told is the will of God for us. In the world-view of the Bible, the will of God is the equivalent of what we would call today the nature or essence of things. The stories of Genesis 1 through 11 are telling us, then, who we are on earth. As such, it would be gravely false to describe them as myths or to feel we could simply substitute this set of stories for others—for what they purport to tell us, taking them on their own terms, is how things "are."

What the opening chapters of Genesis set forth is the paradigm for all human life before Israel came into existence. The "man" and land are said to be intrinsically related. Even if at the time these stories were being written that relationship had become somewhat worn and even partly lost, this basic orientation is said to remain. This is the way it was, Genesis says, and this is the way it should be once again.

In this chapter we will read the opening portion of the Book of Genesis in the light of our contemporary environmental concerns and then listen to a series of homilies upon the days of creation by an eminent Church Father of the West, St. Ambrose. Ambrose will enlighten us both as to how Christians understood Genesis in his day, and also misunderstood it from their particular cultural biases. These understandings and misunderstandings will help us discern the meaning of Genesis for us today.

THE BOOK OF GENESIS

A small but growing literature[1] is emerging around environmental themes in the Bible and the Book of Genesis in particular. The aim is not so much to defend the Bible as to seek its help and wisdom as we develop an

ethic to embrace our planet and all that exists upon it.
This is not just another case of *eisegesis*, of reading into
the text one's own concerns, but more often it has been a
necessary task of correcting what now appears to be a
one-sided reading of the scriptures colored by the controversies of a much later age, so that the genuine wisdom
of the scriptures may appear.

Creation and Redemption

The German exegete Gerhard von Rad, for example,
in a famous essay written over fifty years ago, argued that
the scriptures are so preoccupied with the themes of sin
and redemption that the religious meaning of creation
never actually attained the status of an independent doctrine.[2] It is true that Israel's creed emphasized God's
saving deeds on behalf of his people and that Christian
theology became preoccupied with themes of original sin
and Christ's redeeming death, but this is not to say that
there is no creation doctrine in Genesis or that it is
unimportant. On the contrary, there was no need to
make creation a specific and separate article of Israel's
faith because in that faith the making of the universe and
the making of Israel, according to some accounts, were
one and the same.[3] In Psalm 135, for example, Yahweh is
praised for the goodness and power manifested in many
mighty deeds like the summoning of the clouds and the
sending of rain with lightning flashes as well as the
liberation of Israel from Egypt. Similarly in Psalm 136,
Yahweh is to be thanked for his goodness and
faithfulness for the wonders he has worked from the
creation of the world to the donation to Israel of the

promised land. As Genesis teaches, the creation was not just the making of separate beings but the divine establishment of an entire social system, a people with its rulers and codes of conduct, a land to dwell upon and to share. Genesis has as its goal the origin of the peopled universe we all know.

Some commentators, in order to heighten the perceived originality of Israelite religion, have tended to overlook or even suppress continuities between the religion of Israel and the Canaanite culture within which it emerged, putting Yahweh at too great a distance from the nature gods.[4] By doing so they have only fostered still more the mistaken idea that, in the Bible, history and not nature is what matters.

Israel's early cult makes better sense against the mythopoetic background of the religion of Canaan even if we admit the genuine newness of God's revelation to Abraham and Moses. There are numerous examples of how the cult of Yahweh is conspicuously linked with that of the ancient "God of the Fathers," as we see in this crucial passage from the Book of Exodus in which Yahweh reveals his Name to Moses from out of the burning bush:

> "When I come to the people Israel and say to them, 'The God of your fathers sent me to you,' they will say to me, 'What is his name?' What shall I say to them?" And God said to Moses. . . . "This is what you are to say to the Israelites, 'I AM has sent me to you . . . Yahweh, the God of your ancestors, the God of Abraham, the God of Isaac and the God of Jacob has sent me to you. This is my name for all time.'"[5]

The three pilgrimage feasts of later Israel can be cited as examples of how the celebration of historical events was profoundly linked to the cycles of nature that played such a part in the migratory life of Israel's shepherding past. Passover commemorated the deliverance of Israel from slavery in Egypt; Pentecost the giving of the commandments to Moses on Mount Sinai; and Tabernacles, the most spectacular feast when the Temple was illuminated with torches each night, recalled the leafy shelters in which Israel dwelt on their way to the Promised Land. It was no accident, but intrinsic to the meaning of each, that Passover was a spring festival, Pentecost occurred in summer, and Tabernacles at the time of the fall harvest. The waxing and waning of the moon determined the time for each.

Humanity's Religious Uniqueness

The first of the two creation stories in Genesis emerged from the "priestly" tradition. According to this story, the creation is structured into a week of six days of divine activity concluding on a seventh day of divine rest, when God observed the Sabbath as prescribed in the law of Moses. In this story also the first human couple are created on the sixth day. In the other, more ancient story of the creation, which in Genesis is simply given side by side with the first, with no attempt to harmonize their details, Adam is made first, and there are no "days" of creation. Whether they are said to be made last or first, however, the specialness of human beings is thus portrayed in both.

Here is what God did upon the sixth day, according to the priestly version:

God said, "Let us make man in our own image, in the likeness of ourselves, and let them be masters of the fish of the sea, the birds of heaven, the cattle, all the wild animals and all the creatures that creep along the ground." God created him, male and female he created them. God blessed them, saying to them, "Be fruitful, multiply, fill the earth and subdue it. Be masters of the fish of the sea, the birds of heaven and all the living creatures that move on earth." God also said, "Look, to you I give all the seed-bearing plants everywhere on the surface of the earth, and all the trees with seed-bearing fruits; this will be your food. And to all the wild animals, all the birds of heaven and all the living creatures that creep along the ground, I give all the foliage of the plants as their food." And so it was. God saw all he had made, and indeed it was very good.[6]

A note of sheer delight on the part of God the Creator can be detected as God proudly surveys his work. Again and again in the creation story God is said to see all that he has made and to pronounce it "very good." Part of that goodness is the natural opulence and generosity of the creation, mirroring in this respect the goodness of the One who made it. In this joyous society the first man and woman occupy a central place, but in continuity with the other creatures which similarly have received sexual differentiation and the blessing of fertility. No killing of other animals is allowed, even for the purposes of food and sustenance, by any of the creatures including humanity.

The exact meaning of the word "good" as a description of the world is not certain, but surely it implies that the creation is not merely a functional place but has an aesthetic quality about it, that it is well shaped and ordered, that it is something beautiful.

The theologian John Macquarrie discovers possible artistic nuances in the word for "create" (bara') in Hebrew. The world then would not be something simply external to God but as an artistic expression manifests the one who made it. We cannot make too much of these ideas, for surely in Hebrew society at that time art was not yet a self-conscious activity and artist and artisan were one and the same.[7]

Only the human pair are made in the divine image. Later interpretations will give a Platonic twist to this passage and locate the divine resemblance in the spiritual soul uniquely given to human beings. In Hebrew culture "image" means a "stand-in," one who "represents" another who is greater, as a tiny statuette may be said to represent a king.[8] Human beings are thus to function as God's surrogates in the midst of his creation. They do so by exercising "dominion" over the rest of the creation, but always consciously as God's creatures themselves and accountable to him. In fact, this is part of the human distinctiveness, that humans alone are conscious of their creaturely status. Psalm 8 is a classic utterance in this regard:

> I look up to the heavens, shaped by your fingers, at the moon and the stars you set firm—what are human beings that you spare a thought for them, or the child of Adam that you care for him? Yet you have made him little less than a god, you have crowned him with glory and beauty, made him lord of the works of your hands, put all things under his feet.[9]

But even as in faithfulness to the meaning of Genesis we situate human life within the broader society of life with the other creatures where it naturally finds its proper place, we cannot fail to underscore, also in fidelity to Genesis even in an age of environmental concern, what is one of the most distinctive, and some even say shocking, of its teachings, namely, that human life uniquely is made in the divine "image and likeness." Such a teaching is especially unusual in a religious society that prohibited so strictly any representation of the divine being. It is surely original among the religious beliefs of other Mesopotamian cultures for which, in their creation myths, the human person is the plaything, the slave of the gods, the frightened inhabitant of a menacing natural world. For Genesis, humanity is a dialog partner of God and is given the prerogative reserved to royal personages to exercise dominion in the divine name.

The whole basis of subsequent teaching by the church on social questions of our day revolves around the bedrock conviction of the dignity and inalienable rights of individual persons, a conviction which finds its very basis in the divine creation of humanity in God's own image and likeness. Pope Leo XIII, in accordance with this conviction, declared in his encyclical *Rerum novarum* of 1891 that "the human person precedes the State." In 1961, John XXIII in his encyclical *Mater et Magistra* summarized the development of this teaching thus far in saying, "The cardinal point of this teaching is that individual women and men are necessarily the foundation, cause and end of all social institutions. We are referring to human beings insofar as they are social by nature, raised to an order of existence which transcends and subdues nature.[10] The dignity of the human person, his/her transcendence from the cycles of nature and a "tooth-and-jowl existence," the inviolability of his/her conscience, human rights that are not the gift of the totalitarian state but of God—all of these basic understandings of the human person that are the foundation stones of modern civilization can be traced to the belief that Adam, the one who was made "of the earth," and is therefore "earthy," bears also the divine image. In speaking therefore, as we must, of the limits of human domination and even of the "rights" of other creatures, we must never do so in a way which blurs the real distinction between human life and every other kind of life.

Humanity's Dominion over the Divine Creation

It is around the two related descriptions of humanity as created in God's image and as having dominion over the rest of the creation and subduing it, that the religious understanding of the human person has been based. It is also around these two biblical teachings that so much contemporary controversy has swirled arising out of environmental concerns. Is the Bible perpetuating a misguided anthropocentrism as well as encouraging the continued human exploitation of the planet?

Since human dominion over the creation is to be carried out on behalf of God and is accountable to him, the divine rule becomes the norm of human behavior in this regard. Understood in this way, to have dominion emerges as "to care for," not to manipulate and to exploit. The Lord rules in the Bible not whimsically but "with justice," striking down the oppressor and vindicating the rights of the oppressed.[11] The naming of the animals, which is given to humanity in the second creation story, becomes a symbol not of a power relationship but of a social one. When the flood occurs and wipes out the creation that it may begin anew, the just man Noah is to bring with him onto the ark not only other humans but also representative couples of all the animals, whether they are "useful" to him or not.[12] Humanity thus is seen as savior of the creatures entrusted to them.

Even more fundamentally, the animals join Noah in the ark and in the renewed creation because it is obviously inconceivable to the writer of Genesis that there be human life without animal life. The blessing which God gives to inaugurate the world after the flood is a single blessing for all his creatures, human and non-human. God pledges himself never again to destroy the earth, and the sign of this first of all the covenants, and the most universal, is to be the unchanging succession of the seasons of the year, year after year, the expression of his constant and faithful love. God furthermore places a rainbow in the sky as a reminder (to himself!) that the earth shall never be destroyed again.[13] Inanimate nature thus joins the animals and humanity as joint recipients of the divine blessing and pledge. Humanity and the animals are partners in a single covenant.

In spite of the disasters that humanity has brought upon the original creation, God reconfirms human dominion after the flood. In recognition now of the facts of history, humanity may kill other living creatures for food, but the blood is to be reserved to indicate that God alone is the Lord of life.[14] The "peaceable kingdom," envisioned by the prophet Isaiah,[15] where "the wolf will live with the lamb, the panther lie down with the kid; calf, lion and cattle browse together, with a little child to lead them," thus becomes a dream of some future time that harkens back to the harmonies of God's original creation.

The Bible of course does not use philosophical definitions, but if we were to define human nature in a philosophical mode out of biblical teaching it would be in the terms of the divine command to the first humans, "Be fruitful, multiply and fill the earth and subdue it. Be masters of the fish of the sea, the birds of the heavens and all the living creatures that move on the earth."[16] To procreate and to take the land—this twofold task is what it means to be a human being according to Genesis. It is true that in Hebrew to "subdue" has violent overtones, and that its equivalent would be found in a phrase such as "to trample one's enemy under one's feet."[17] Such a violent activity may seem more appropriate if we consider that it is the first inhabitation by humans of a wilderness that is being described. But a more adequate understanding of the term emerges when we understand it as meaning to occupy and develop that special portion of the land which God has given to each tribe or people.

According to the Book of Deuteronomy, God established the divisions of humankind and gave all nations their lands and their proper boundaries.[18] The peopling of the earth by different clans as thus described in Genesis follows the assignment by God to each of a particular place in which to live. God's anger flares when certain peoples refuse to inhabit their proper place, deciding instead to build a tower "reaching to the heavens."[19] God then scatters them, that is, sends them back to where they belong.

The land given to Israel, according to a subsequent account, will be the land of Canaan; this is the land they are to "subdue" upon the command of God. But this is part of later history. In the first part of Genesis attention is given to the common origins and destination of all humanity. But even in Genesis we are made to understand that "to subdue the land" means to occupy and develop the land God has given each; it does not mean to exploit it in greed and violence. "To subdue" means to receive a divine gift.

What really emerges then in the divine creation is not merely the physical universe but the world of women and men, a whole society of organized relationships and kinship systems. According to the Hebrew notion of wisdom, that most elusive of virtues, we are to learn and respect how these systems work, not disrupt and destroy them. We must learn our "place."

But, as Genesis reports, humanity lacked such wisdom. In what is no doubt one of the saddest sentences in the entire Bible, coming so unexpectedly after the repeated declarations of how good God found everything he made, God is said to have "regretted having made human beings upon the earth and was grieved to the heart."[20] Nature and humanity are to be destroyed together because they form a single overlapping world. Nonhuman phenomena as reported in the Bible are often reciprocal to human activity, as in the heavenly and earthly signs that often accompany portentious events.[21]

By contrast, nature for the Greeks was "dead"; only humans were "alive." Thus the modern term for landscape painting is "nature morte." The Newtonian conception of nature as a machine is not far from such a conception. In the biblical world-view, however, nature is not dead but alive. All the animals as well as humanity receive the divine "breath." The aliveness of nature may

be seen in a typical passage from the Hebrew psalms
that really has no counterpart in Greek sources:

> Let the sea roar and all that fills it resound,
> the world and those that dwell therein!
> Let the floods clap their hands,
> let the hills sing for joy together
> before the Lord, for he comes
> to judge the earth.[22]

Out of the same world-view, Paul in the Letter to the
Romans speaks of the whole of creation waiting with
eager longing for the revelation of the children of God,
for the creation itself has been held in the same frustration as humanity itself. The whole of creation has been
"groaning with labor pains" until now, awaiting its
glorious freedom, the same glorious freedom as the children of God.[23]

There is then no sharp distinction between humanity
and nature, but a common participation in life. Nature is
the human environment.[24]

Whie the Greeks viewed nature in terms of "act and
potency," something that could be changed by human
ingenuity, the Hebrews as part of the "Eternal East"
tended to regard nature as something given and
changeless. Human manipulation of the natural order,
therefore, was completely foreign to the Hebrew com-
prehension of our place in the world.

Not only is there a unity of humanity and nature, but
humanity itself is united in a single place and destiny.
Eve, the "mother of all those who live,"[25] plunges humanity into a common catastrophe by her disobedience

and deception. The genealogies of Genesis, which are so carefully constructed, were of great interest to the ancients as situating them within the history of the world and its peoples. When the world receives a new beginning and a new common ancestor in Noah, his three sons, Shem, Ham, and Japheth, were considered to represent all the world.[26]

The land belonging to the Lord is given in perpetuity to certain peoples and nations, but never loses its relationship to God, the primary "owner." Thus in Joshua 13, the land is distributed by lot, that is, by divine intent. Naboth in First Kings considers it out of the question to sell his ancestral inheritance even to a king for a fair price. Queen Jezebel simply cannot understand this, that an ancestral inheritance can never be merely a piece of property to be bought and sold.[27]

The "year of jubilee," as described in Leviticus and Deuteronomy, during which lands that had become alienated were to be returned to their original owners, whether it was practiced very much or not, is another expression of the same truth—that the land is the Lord's to dispose of. In the Song of the Vineyard of Isaiah 5, it is stated that there is no right to make large holdings out of small parcels. The suspicion of Israel toward the institution of kingship shows a similar perspective which is very different from that of other Near Eastern societies. The Lord is the ultimate ruler, and that shows where true sovereignty and ownership lie.

The faith of the ancient Psalms is expressed in Genesis and the other books of the Hexateuch. It is a faith that invites the whole natural world to join humanity in offering a prayer of praise and thanksgiving to God for the marvels he has wrought in his magnificent creation.

You crown the year with your generosity,
richness seeps from your tracks,
the pastures of the desert grow moist,
the hillsides are wrapped in joy,
the meadows are covered with flocks,
the valleys clothed with wheat;
they shout and sing for joy.[28]

ST. AMBROSE ON GENESIS

St. Ambrose (about A.D. 339–97), the learned and aristocratic bishop of Milan, provided the other preeminent Church Father of the West, St. Augustine (A.D. 354–430) with the conceptual key that would allow Augustine to become a Christian: the preeminence of spirit over matter. In doing so, Peter Brown claims in his biography of Augustine, Ambrose allowed Augustine to make an intellectual breakthrough that "is a decisive and fateful step in the evolution of our ideas on spirit and matter."[29]

Among the many sermons of Ambrose, delivered with impressive oratorical skill, that Augustine most likely heard in the cathedral of Milan were those on the Book of Genesis. In them Augustine would have heard ideas that struck him as revolutionary, given his materialist background as a Manichaean. "I noticed, repeatedly, in the sermons of our bishop," Augustine later reflected, "that when God is thought of, our thoughts should dwell on no material reality whatsoever, nor in the case of the soul, which is the one thing in the universe nearest to God."[30]

Otherworldliness was the consistent theme of Ambrose's Christianity. Our bodies are mere "garments"[31] for our souls, our true selves. Learned in Greek, Ambrose made abundant use of the exegetical tools developed by Philo of Alexandria (about 20 B.C.–A.D. 50) and employed by the Greek Fathers to find a more elevated and spiritual meaning behind the rather pedestrian events of God's dealings with Israel. Philo's project of reconciling Judaism and Hellenism through a spiritual reading of the Hebrew scriptures was not dissimilar to the rereading by the Greek philosophers of Homer and his embarrassingly naive myths. Philo applied their allegorical method to the Old Testament itself. Gregory of Nyssa (about 335–95) interpreted the Pauline utterance, "The letter kills, the spirit gives life" to mean that the life-giving message of scripture can only be found beneath and behind the literal letter of its narrative. This became the dominant theme of Ambrose's preaching: "Beneath the opaque and rebarbative 'letter' of the Old Testament, this 'spirit,' the hidden meaning, calls to our spirit to rise and fly away into another world."[32] It was precisely this method of interpretation that made it possible for Augustine to regard the patriarchs in a different light. "What had once appeared to him, when a Manichee, as a collection of formidable and disgusting *bons pères de famille*, were presented by Ambrose as a stately procession of authentic 'philosophers' each one symbolizing the state of a soul purified by wisdom."[33]

Ambrose begins his series of homilies on the six days of creation by referring to an array of pagan philosophers, Plato first among them all, whose various and conflicting views about the origin of things he will contrast with the serene surety of Moses who had the incomparable advantage of speaking with God himself, face to face. According to Philo, Plato ("the most holy Plato" he calls him) developed his philosophy as an offshoot from the same divine revelation given to Moses. In a similar fashion Ambrose turns Moses into a kind of Platonic philosopher, learned in all areas of secular knowledge and withdrawing from earthly pursuits to practice contemplation.[34] Moses, according to Ambrose, "foresaw" the errors of later philosophers and refuted their "vain errors" by his creation accounts. God alone is the Creator of the heavens and the earth at the beginning of time. Matter does not participate in the divinity; God, and God alone, is eternal and what he creates he creates with full freedom.

Reading these homilies today they seem still what they no doubt were to their first hearers and to Augustine: not speculative theology but the conscientious and learned exposition of scripture by a pastoral bishop concerned about the eternal salvation of his flock. In their amplitude, there is room for an excursus on the glories of the sea[35] (Ambrose chides himself for this digression among many others) and for direct moral applications. Ambrose, for example, contrasts the prompt obedience of the rest of creation to divine commands with the less-than-admirable performance of his hearers in attending the weekly eucharistic celebration in the Lord's house.[36] There is space too for an occasional prayer.

As a learned and patriotic Roman, Ambrose marshalls numerous citations from the classic authors—Virgil, Cicero, Lucretius, Horace—to fill out his glowing account of the splendors of the earth and the creatures that fill it as they all come forth from the bountiful hand of their Creator. The worshipers who are commended for gathering in church in preference to the theater display, according to Ambrose, a proper awe and reverence for the creation.

> Here are people who find no delight in tapestries of purple or costly stage curtains. Their pleasure lies rather in their admiration of this most beautiful fabric of the world, this accord of unlike elements, this heaven that is spread out like a tent to dwell in to protect those who inhabit this world. They find their pleasure in the earth allotted to them for their labors, in the ambient air, in the seas here enclosed in their bounds. In the people who are the instruments of the operations of God they hear music which echoes from melodious sound of God's word, within which the Spirit of God works.[37]

Birds, fish, trees, plants, animals—all receive extended admiration in all their species and kinds. A description of the grapevine leads to a discussion of the joys of wine and finally to a meditation upon our true citizenship which is in heaven, suggested by the vine's upward ascent.[38] Nothing, Ambrose notes, is without its purpose, nothing superfluous.[39]

Ambrose goes on, as indeed he must, to describe the admirable qualities of the human body and expresses appreciation for the tenderness of a kiss:

> What shall I say of the kiss which is a symbol of affection and love? Doves exchange kisses, but what is this compared to the charm of a kiss of a human being in which the note of friendliness and kind-

liness is conspicuous, and where is expressed the indubitable sense of our sincerest affection?[40]

But Ambrose reserves his highest praise for the human soul. "Our soul," he declares, "is made to the image of God. It is our entire essence, because without it we are nothing but earth and into the earth we shall return. . . . Your soul is made to the image of God, whereas your body is related to the beasts."[41] As he concludes his homilies upon the days of creation, Ambrose meditates upon the divine rest, a rest, he says, which God took in the recesses of the human soul:

> I give thanks to our Lord God, who made a work of such a nature that he could find rest therein. He made the heavens. I do not read that he rested. He made the earth. I do not read that he rested. He made the sun, moon and stars. I do not read that he found rest there. But I do read that he made the human person and then found rest in one whose sins he would remit.[42]

Though the soul is elevated over the material body, the body itself cannot be called evil. Human sins account for the evil in the world, according to Ambrose, and not materiality as the "deadly pest of the Manichaeans" asserts. "Evil is not a living substance but a deviation of the mind and soul away from the path of virtue. Our adversary is within us."[43]

Many unresolved issues that Ambrose did not pursue in his synthesis of scripture and secular culture were left to Augustine to confront. "Ambrose," according to Peter

Brown, "was not as clever as Augustine: and he was very much the traditional, educated bishop of his time. For him, the main problem was still to understand the 'spiritual' message of the Old Testament in terms of allegories evolved by the Alexandrian school."[44] When a negative reaction to Origen began to set in, the Alexandrian school accordingly began to lose favor. A new synthesis was needed. Augustine in his industry and genius succeeded in going beyond not only his prior Manichaean beliefs but also, in some significant ways, the Neoplatonism of his time. Through his deepening insight into Christian revelation he saw the need to keep body and soul literally together. Margaret Miles writes: "Not only modern commentators, but also medieval followers of Augustine have ignored the overwhelming contextual evidence of his struggle to integrate the body and to understand the implications of embodied experience."[45] Miles sees Augustine's thought developing from a treatment of the body as a *foil* for the soul, to a *problem* for the soul, and finally to the human body as simply the *condition* of human learning, trial, and ultimate victory.[46]

Robin Lane Fox comments on Augustine's debt to Ambrose and his evolution beyond Ambrose:

> Like Gregory, Augustine had left a distant province in search of a pagan education. Away from home, he, too, had coincided with a great Christian teacher: Ambrose was to be his Origen, Milan his Caesarea. Augustine, too, returned home to rapid promotion as a bishop and a life of hard, practical rule over a flock who knew only too well how to sin.

> In this life, the contacts with Ambrose and his philosophic culture gave way to the bedrock of Scripture and the Old Testament.[47]

In an unconscious way, Ambrose, too, was expressing the same view. He may have been writing off intellectually all of the creation except the human soul as simply "flesh," but reading his homilies upon the days of creation there is no question where his heart and affections lay—clearly upon the earth. In another series of homilies, Ambrose offered more hope for the world: "In Christ's resurrection the world arose, in Christ's resurrection the heavens arose, in Christ's resurrection the earth itself arose."[48] The present form of the world passes away in its wretchedness, but the world itself endures to be changed into a better form, one destined for eternity. Ambrose like other Church Fathers sought to spiritualize the meaning of the Bible, but even in their spiritual interpretations and free associations between and within the two Testaments they were always saved by their adherence to the literal text. It was the literal text which was divinely inspired and so it had to be the basis of everything.

In the end, the scandalous particularity of divine revelation could not be done away with. For the Bible, unlike other religious systems, historical truth and the everyday reality of its narrative are intrinsic to its meaning, because it claims to provide sacred ordinances for our actual life on earth. The Bible is not in the genre of a fiction helping us to forget for a while the reality of our life but rather aims to assist us actually to see our reality as part of sacred history. Its very ordinariness, its "mate-

riality," is thus the Bible's spirituality; reality is not portrayed there as something closed in on itself, but also not
as something other than itself. As Erich Auerbach has
written, "The sublime influence of God here reaches so
deeply into the everyday that the two realms of the
sublime and the everyday are not only actively unsepa-
rated but basically inseparable."[49]

In the vibrant mosaics of the churches of Ravenna we
may see a world not far removed from that of Ambrose's
homilies. Creation and new creation blend there into
each other. In one depiction, Christ the Good Shepherd
appears amid mystic yet realistic sheep, surrounded by
birds, flowers, and various animals abounding beneath a
star-filled sky. The background consists of watery greens
and blues that suggest both the sea that Ambrose loved
so much as well as the saving cascade of baptism. In the
church of San Vitale there is in the triumphal arch a
mosaic head of Christ encircled with Noah's rainbow.
Outside this luminous ring there swim in adoration
green dolphins streaked with yellow and red, God's kingdom come upon earth!

5 GENESIS APPLIED BY POPE JOHN PAUL II

As we look to religious tradition for a wisdom to guide our life on earth, the Book of Genesis has unique value. Pope John Paul II has certainly found it so. He discovers within it not only the divine charge to use all the resources of human intelligence and industry for the full development of the world entrusted to us but also fundamental ethical standards according to which this development is to occur. Such standards, he declares, are based "according to the Creator's original ordering"[1] as disclosed both by rational reflection and the light of faith. Pope John Paul has a fascination with this particular book of the Bible. He has returned to it again and again in his speeches and writings. This fascination no doubt comes from the deeply held conviction that the human person, in all the details of our concrete, historical existence, is for him "the way" for the church;[2] for between the saving, eschatological purpose of the church and concern for our earthly life there are bonds that are "unbreakable."[3]

His seventh and most recent encyclical letter, *Sollicitudo rei socialis* ("Concern for Social Matters"), and its applications of Genesis and subsequent church tradition to environmental concerns, will be the focus of this chapter. The occasion for this letter was the twentieth anniversary of the publication of *Populorum progressio* ("On the Progress of Peoples") by his predecessor, Paul VI. That encyclical was written out of a passionate concern for the full possibility for development by all the peoples of the world, especially those peoples chronically designated "underdeveloped." "Development is the new name for peace," Paul VI had said.[4]

For his part, John Paul admits that the term "development" is taken from the social and economic sciences, and at first glance development seems "extraneous to the legitimate concern of the church seen as a religious institution."[5] But, he goes on, it is not extraneous if we understand the meaning of religion, especially as it has been elaborated in the social teaching of the church over the past 100 years.

That social teaching, as we have seen, was given an enormous boost by the Second Vatican Council and especially its pastoral constitution *Gaudium et spes*. John Paul II had a hand in developing portions of that constitution, and in particular its early anthropological sections. As a professional philosopher who continued his academic pursuits even as a bishop and cardinal, he has been preoccupied with questions related to the dignity of the human person.[6] As pope, John Paul regards the Second Vatican Council as the ecclesial event of our time and its implementation the primary goal of his pontificate.

Encyclicals are official teachings of popes addressed to the universal church and, more recently, to all the peoples of the world. John Paul has written three of them which deal significantly with social concerns: *Redemptor hominis,* his inaugural encyclical as pope; *Laborem exer-cens,* written in 1981; and now *Sollicitudo rei socialis,* dated for the end of December 1987, but issued in February 1988.

The reactions to this latest papal encyclical, positive and negative, have been unusually strong. It was not just that the pope appeared to be wandering far from strictly religious matters as some conceive them; it was that John Paul seemed also to be too sweeping in his criticism of existing social and political arrangements. He lays blame upon both East and West, Marxist collectivism and Western capitalism, and their continuing conflicts and competition, for the underdevelopment of peoples who are reduced to being "parts of a machine, cogs in a gigantic wheel."[7] But even more unsettling was his insistence, based upon Genesis, upon the strictly conditioned right of private property as deduced from the universal designation by the Creator of all things for the common good. "Private property, in fact, is under a social mortgage,"[8] he states forcefully. This teaching seemed to undermine the very foundations of capitalism concerning the irrevocable right of private ownership based upon legitimate acquisition. The pope instead was speaking about another right, the balancing right of entitlement by humanity to the necessities of life. Whatever one's position on this matter, it is a good example of the contemporary relevance of a proper reading and application of the Book of Genesis and the uncomfortable adjustments in thinking and living that may be required.

The right to private property is so engrained in Western political thought that some have alleged that John Paul, coming from an Eastern socialist country, fails to understand its import as a basis for political and economic freedoms. They go on to say that it is the Western capitalist democracies, which have given the private sector sufficient freedom from government intrusion, that allow such institutions as churches to carry out their charitable activities. But this, of course, is the whole point. John Paul, and the whole tradition of Catholic social teaching out of which he speaks, is not concerned only with allowing private agencies to dispense charity. He raises and it raises the issue of justice. "Peace is the fruit of justice," he cites the tradition as saying. And, in this latest encyclical, he adds to that tradition his own particular contribution which may be said to draw its remote inspiration from the Book of Genesis: "Peace is the fruit of solidarity."[9]

Before discussing the encyclical's principal points, we will survey other allusions to Genesis by John Paul that will provide a context for what he says in this latest writing. In doing so it will become clearer that while he is making his own original contribution especially from his personalist perspective, what he is saying is consistent with long-standing biblical and Christian principles.

John Paul's personalist perspective has caused him to be faulted for an exclusively anthropocentric approach to social questions,[10] but his intention, frequently stated, is to unite and never separate anthropocentrism and theocentrism—the centrality of the human person and the centrality of God. The one for him implies and requires the other for its truth. The overcoming of their separation, he has claimed, was one of the principal achievements, if not *the* principal achievement, of the Second Vatican Council.[11] This too is only in keeping with Genesis where the central role of the human person opens up into the still broader perspective of God the Creator of all things, human and nonhuman.

PRIOR APPLICATIONS OF GENESIS

It is to be expected that a modern pope's inaugural encyclical will be programmatic of his entire pontificate. This was never more true than in the case of John Paul II, who plays a major part in the composition of his principal writings. In *Redemptor hominis* ("The Redeemer of Humanity") John Paul announces the principal themes that have found expression in numerous other forms ever since. One major theme is surely the affirmation that "the God of the creation and the God of the redemption are one God."[12] In fact, according to John Paul, it is in Christ the Redeemer that there has been revealed "in a new and more wonderful way the fundamental truth concerning creation to which the Book of Genesis gives witness when it repeats several times: 'God saw that it was good.'"[13]

Redemptor hominis continues, referring to St. Paul's use of Genesis in the Letter to the Romans:

Are we of the twentieth century not convinced of the overpoweringly eloquent words of the apostle to the gentiles concerning the "creation [that] has been groaning in travail together until now" and "waits with eager longing for the revelation of the sons of God," the creation that "was subjected to futility"?[14] Does not the previously unknown immense progress which has taken place especially in the course of this century in the field of human dominion over the world itself reveal—to a previously unknown degree—that manifold subjection "to futility"? It is enough to recall certain phenomena, such as the threat of pollution of the natural environment in areas of rapid industrialization, or the armed conflicts continually breaking out over and over again, or the prospect of self-destruction through the use of atomic, hydrogen, neutron and similar weapons, or the lack of respect for the life of the unborn. The world of the new age, the world of space flights, the world of the previously unattained conquests of science and technology—is it not also the world "groaning in travail" that "waits with eager longing for the revealing of the sons of God"?[15]

John Paul, who is of a mystic bent, sees in the cross of Christ, God's "leaving" this world and at the same time giving a fresh manifestation of his eternal fatherhood by the outpouring of his Spirit, drawing near once again.[16] Human dignity has been restored, and the name "for' that deep amazement at human worth and dignity is the Gospel."[17] Besides *Redemptor hominis,* a series of audience talks and the encyclical *Laborem exercens* ("On Human Labor") are the paramount examples before *Sollicitudo* of John Paul's applications of Genesis to contemporary ethical concerns.

Beginning in September 1979 and continuing through the spring of 1981, John Paul gave a remarkable series of weekly addresses at his Wednesday audiences on the theme of the body. His principal source was the Book of Genesis. The first human, John Paul states, is profoundly aware of being "alone" in the midst of creation, of being "different" from those beings to which he has given their names. "Actually, the first man might have concluded," John Paul goes on, "on the basis of his experience of his own body, that he was substantially similar to other living beings; instead, however, he concluded he was 'alone' with his Creator, he alone is a partner with the Absolute." He is the image of God.

It is actually in the communion of the two sexes, male and female, that the human person became the image and likeness of God, according to John Paul, Masculinity and femininity are two different "incarnations," two ways of "being a body," two ways of being "in the image of God."[18] This point of exegesis troubled the Church Fathers. Augustine certainly was more positive than his culture and contemporaries when he interpreted Genesis to mean that woman as well as man was created in the divine image, but not, he would say, as woman or in the body of either, but in the soul. Commentators stress that it is the "intention" of Augustine that is important here, more than his "content,"[19] an intention which John Paul develops to the fullest. In Matthew 19, John Paul says, Jesus appeals to this social image of God in male and female at the beginning as a model of true communion of persons united in one flesh. Communion is thus revealed as the deepest reality of life, human and divine.

In 1981 Pope John Paul wrote his encyclical *Laborem exercens*, on the ninetieth anniversary of Leo XIII's *Rerum novarum* ("Of New Things") that had inaugurated the modern phase of the church's social teaching. But, as the pope points out, "the question goes back much further than the last ninety years. In fact the church's social teaching finds its source in Sacred Scripture, beginning with the Book of Genesis and especially in the Gospel and the writings of the apostles."[20] The whole document is inspired by two key verses from Genesis: The human person is made in the image and likeness of God[21] and is placed in the world in order to subdue the earth.[22] "These words," he writes, "placed at the beginning of the Bible, *never cease to be relevant*" (original emphasis).[23] No prior papal encyclical on social questions had ever made Genesis so central to its development.

In these passages the pope finds what he calls "*a key, probably the essential key,* to the whole social question," namely human work.[24] "The human person is the image of God partly through the mandate received from the Creator to subdue, to dominate, the earth. In carrying out this mandate, every human being reflects the very action of the Creator of the universe."[25] The pope then in an original way distinguishes work in an objective sense ("the products of human labor") from work in a subjective sense (as a self-actualization of the one who works in fulfillment of a divine vocation). John Paul gives preeminence to work in its subjective meaning[26] and asserts "the priority of labor over capital."[27]

From these assertions two conclusions follow. The ethical aspects of work are revealed especially in its subjective dimension, which means that work must never become merchandise, for it is the expression and fulfillment of the person who is working.[28] The other conclusion, in opposition to both collectivism and capitalism, is that private ownership of capital, while legitimate within certain limits, is subordinated to the right of common use of the goods of creation.[29] Justice and solidarity are thus the prevailing ethical categories for the evaluation of economic life.

There is one reference by John Paul in *Laborem exer-*

cens to environmental concerns; he notes "the growing realization that the heritage of nature is limited and that it is being intolerably polluted."[30] The context of this reference is with regard to new developments in technology, economic and political life, developments which generally are taken for granted by the pope who sees them as constituting a new moral challenge.

The biblical exegete Claus Westermann, in his commentary on Genesis, also stresses the ethical meaning of the divine charge to humanity to "dominate." The Hebrew verb, he explains, is "used particularly of the rule of kings. According to the ancient view, however, there is no suggestion of exploitation; on the contrary, the king is personally responsible for the well-being and prosperity of those he rules."[31] A kingly rule, actually, is not far from John Paul's conception of human work as the activity of someone endowed with a divinely given dignity.

SOLLICITUDO REI SOCIALIS ("CONCERN FOR SOCIAL MATTERS")

What *Laborem exercens* lacked, according to some commentators, was a more detailed global analysis to fill out its striking social doctrine.[32] This is precisely what *Sollicitudo rei socialis* supplies, picking up on the central assertion of *Populorum progressio:* "Today the principal fact that we must all recognize is that the social question has become world-wide."[33] In it John Paul demonstrates the numerous ways that the East-West conflict has heightened the development gap between the peoples of the North and South.

The environmental theme also receives its fullest

treatment in this encyclical. It lists "among today's positive signs" ecological concern, "a greater realization of the limits of available resources and the need to respect the integrity and cycles of nature when planning for development."[34] More importantly, the letter provides three considerations regarding the respect that is due from humanity to the cosmos, a term deliberately chosen because in its precise meaning cosmos refers to an order existing independently of us. These three are: "One cannot use with impunity the different categories of beings, whether living or inanimate—animals, plants, the natural elements—simply as one wishes, according to one's own economic needs, without taking into account the nature of each being and its mutual connection in an ordered system . . . natural resources are limited and some are not renewable . . . the direct or indirect result of industrialization is, ever more frequently, the pollution of the environment, with serious consequences for the health of the population."[35]

John Paul concludes his direct treatment of environmental issues by applying another passage from the Book of Genesis: "The dominion granted to humanity by the Creator is not an absolute power nor can one speak of a freedom to 'use and misuse' or to dispose of things as one pleases. The limitation imposed from the beginning by the Creator himself and expressed symbolically by the prohibition not to 'eat of the fruit of the tree'[36] shows clearly enough that, when it comes to the natural world, we are subject not only to biological laws but also to moral ones, which cannot be violated with impunity."[37]

The divine likeness which humanity bears calls us to "cultivate the garden" of the world by seeing to its and our full development, but always in accordance with this divine likeness. The divine likeness is both transcendent, inasmuch as it points beyond this world, and social, referring to human society. "When the human disobeys God and refuses to submit to his rule," John Paul states, "nature rebels against him and no longer recognizes him as its 'master,' for he has tarnished the divine image in himself."[38]

Still, even after the "fall," John Paul declares that the story of the human race described by scripture is a story of "constant achievements," though always threatened by sin. He continues:

> Here the perspectives widen. The dream of "un-limited progress" reappears, radically transformed by the new outlook created by Christian faith, as-suring us that progress is possible only because God the Father has decided from the beginning to make humanity a sharer of his glory in Jesus Christ risen from the dead. . . . In him God wished to conquer sin and make it serve our greater good, which infi-nitely surpasses what progress could achieve.
>
> We can say therefore—as we struggle amid the obscurities and deficiencies of underdevelopment and superdevelopment—that one day this corrupti-ble body will put on incorruptibility, this mortal body immortality (cf. 1 Cor 15:54) when the Lord "delivers the kingdom to God the Father" (v. 24) and all the works and actions of humanity will be re-deemed.[39]

The encyclical *Sollicitudo rei socialis* holds greatest interest in the last of its five sections, the one entitled, "A Theological Reading of Modern Problems." After sum-marizing Pope Paul's encyclical, surveying world condi-tions today, and evaluating them in terms of the requirements of authentic human development, John Paul outlines pivotal points of the church's social teaching as it has developed and is still developing. He sees in this teaching principles for reflection, criteria for judgment, as well as directives for action. The social teaching fundamentally establishes that our developing life is not merely a technical problem to be solved but requires moral reflection and evaluation. It is decidedly not just another ideology, a "third way" between liberal capitalism and Marxist collectivism, but a behavioral guide in the carrying out of our vocation which is at once "earthly and transcendent."[40]

For our purposes, in this concluding section of *Sollicitudo*, John Paul gives us three guiding principles of immense value in facing the ethical issues that are confronting us on a worldwide scale and across national frontiers. These are: the principle of solidarity, that is to say, the great network of interdependence that exists among us all[41]; the universal destination of the goods of the earth; and, implicitly, a third principle, that human reasoning among persons of good will, even if they do not profess the same religious faith, can disclose norms for ethical life, a process sometimes described as "the natural law." It is to these three principles that we now turn. All find their roots in Genesis, and even though, in the elaboration of John Paul, they are more directly applied to humanity, indirectly and by inference they encompass everything that coexists with us on this planet.

Solidarity

The image of God in humanity is a social one, according to John Paul.[42] Life in communion and solidarity with others is the divine model for all earthly existence. A sense of world community, membership in the family of humankind, and the common good are its expressions.

Life in solidarity is not a middle position between individualism and collectivism, but "a new and unique approach to human relationships emphasizing personal dignity and our social nature as human beings."[43] This ontic and ethical principle of mutual responsibility is found in the Book of Genesis. It extends beyond the human community to the rest of creation over which humanity exercises dominion.[44]

The reverse of solidarity is what John Paul calls the erection of a "structure of sin," the fruit of many personal sins. Two such structures he specifies are "the all-consuming desire for profit and the thirst for power . . . at any price."[45] Conversion is required, conversion of attitude from selfishness to servanthood, to love of neighbor, especially of the poorest neighbor.[46]

For John Paul, solidarity is a moral and social attitude, a virtue to be practiced, a duty to be expressed. It has a worldwide dimension. It is more than feelings of compassion or distress. It is a firm and persevering determination to commit oneself to the good of all and of each individual, because we are really responsible for all.[47]

The Christian expression of solidarity is communion. Human life finds its deepest expression in the unity of life and love of the divine Trinity.[48] In the scriptures hospitality is listed among the most characteristic virtues of the Christian. When a commentator criticizes that *Sollicitudo* "enshrines the rhetoric of resentment,"[49] he speaks out of a materialist mentality that does not understand the positive vision of life that is being enunciated. The hospitable person unselfconsciously shares what he has because for him the stranger is not a stranger but a guest, a Lazarus at the gate.

We are bold enough to describe the human situation
in the modern world as far removed from the objective demands of the moral order, from the exigen-
cies of justice, and still more, from social love. . . .
This pattern represents the gigantic development of
the parable in the Bible of the rich banqueter and
the poor man Lazarus. So widespread is this phenomenon that it brings into question the financial,
monetary, production and commercial mechanisms
that support the world economy. . . . By submitting
humanity to tensions created by ourselves, di-
lapidating at an accelerated pace material and energy resources, and compromising the geophysical
environment, these structures unceasingly make the
areas of misery spread, accompanied by anguish,
frustration and bitterness.[50]

The opposite of a life based upon sharing, hospitality,
and love is one that John Paul calls the civilization of
consumption or of consumerism, a throwaway society
that wastes and does not see waste as a moral problem.
"An object already owned but now superseded by something better is discarded, with no thought of its possible
lasting value in itself nor of some other human being
who is poorer."[51] It is a society, Paul VI had said, that
thinks that development is having more rather than
being more.

The Universal Destination of the Goods of the Earth

John Paul sees the "duty of solidarity" to lead to the
blessing of peace. "Peoples excluded from the fair distribution of the goods originally destined for all could ask
themselves," he writes, "Why not respond with violence

to those who first treat us with violence?"[52] The presumption here is that the goods of the earth are accepted as originally destined for the good of all, a destination which cannot be cancelled even by lawful acquisition. John Paul cites in this regard a key section of *Populorum progressio*:

"Fill the earth and subdue it" (Gn 1:28): the Bible, from the first page on, teaches us that the whole of creation is for humanity, that it is his/her responsibility to develop it by intelligent effort and by means of his/her labor to perfect it for his/her use. If the world is made to furnish each individual with the means of livelihood and the instruments for growth and progress, each person therefore has the right to find in the world what is necessary for him/herself. The recent council reminded us of this: "God intended the earth and all that it contains for the use of every human being and people. Thus, as all persons follow justice and unite in charity, created goods should abound for them on a reasonable basis" (*Gaudium et spes*, 69). All other rights whatsoever, including those of property and of free commerce, are to be subordinated to this principle. . . . That is, private property does not constitute for anyone an absolute and unconditioned right. No one is justified in keeping for his/her exclusive use what he/she does not need, according to the traditional doctrine as found in the Fathers of the Church and the great theologians, the right to property must never be exercised to the detriment of the common good.[53]

In the philosophical tradition the church employs, the Thomistic concept of the "common good" means the totality of the goods (the rights and duties) of individuals taken together. The common good means that the good of an individual may not be sacrificed for the good of all, for when the good of even a single individual is not respected, the common good itself is not achieved.[54]

In *Laborem exercens* and once again in *Sollicitudo*, John Paul calls "the first principle of the whole ethical and social order" the principle of the common use of goods.[55] Lacking this moral vision, it has fallen to government agencies and large corporate entities to intervene in order to limit the rights of property owners in the interests of environmental protection and other concerns. John Paul does not raise these disturbing questions because he speaks outside the American context. Owing to the lack of moral consensus, great strain has been placed upon traditional legal institutions as well as traditional legal concepts in all Western countries. The mystique of property, as Harold Berman observes, and the concept of nature as property are running up against the realities of the modern social order. The result has been more movement in the direction of centralization and bureaucratization of all aspects of life.[56]

The Natural Law

John Paul points to the appeal by Paul VI to "all persons of good will" and not just to those of the household of the faith as one of the more striking and original features of *Populorum progressio.* John Paul writes:

> One would hope that also men and women without an explicit faith would be convinced that the obstacles to integral development are not only economic

but rest on a more profound attitude which human beings can make into absolute values. Thus one would hope that all those who, to some degree or other, are responsible for ensuring a "more human life" for their fellow human beings, whether or not they are inspired by a religious faith, will become fully aware of the urgent need to change the spiritual attitudes which define each individual's relationship with self, with neighbor, with even the remotest human communities and with nature itself; and all of this in view of higher values such as the common good . . ."[57]

John XXIII had been the first to broaden the audience of a papal encyclical by using this phrase in his final such writing, *Pacem in terris* ("Peace on Earth") issued in 1963. This encyclical, as well as an earlier one on social questions written by John, *Mater et Magistra* ("Mother and Teacher"), drew its ethical principles not only from the Bible and church tradition but also from the principles of the natural law. This was the basis of the appeal to "all persons of good will." Such an appeal is obviously essential in any joint effort to address a problem of such universal scope as the environment.

The natural law as a philosophy antedates Christianity but was given a comfortable place within the Christian synthesis, most notably by Thomas Aquinas. Natural law according to Aquinas is the divine eternal law immanent in the creation, and humanity participates in this law by the use of its unique gift of reason. Although our problematic is different from that of Aquinas who was attempting to reconcile God's providential guidance of all creatures with the possibility of human freedom, natural law does offer possibilities for us today for rational discourse about the limits of human intervention into nature made possible by our intelligence and ingenuity. Such interventions are not necessarily to be rejected immediately simply because they are "artificial" but are to be subjected to some kind of objective moral evaluation.[58] Such an evaluation must take into account the advances in science and culture which have affected our conceptions of what is "natural." It would also involve, for the Christian, the specific orientation and values of divine revelation—but always with the understanding, implicit in the Catholic tradition, that this orientation and these values are susceptible to reasonable analysis and objective evaluation even if they ultimately rest for their validity and force upon a commitment of faith.

The objections to natural law, however, have been frequently stated. The theologian Joseph Sittler faults it as "anthropologically anachronistic."[59] The biologist Edward Wilson rejects any notion "that immutable mandates are placed by God in human nature."[60] The Protestant ethician James M. Gustafson regards natural-law ethics as deficient because it is not based upon divine revelation; coming out of the Reformation tradition, Gustafson has little trust that unaided reason can arrive at truth.[61] Others have commented that precepts of the natural law are too general and too vague to provide adequate norms for behavior.

Several new approaches to natural law are promising, however, and have taken many of these objections into account. A phenomenological analysis based upon natural law, for example, wishes to avoid a false "objectivism" while providing an objective challenge to existing legal

systems and social arrangements. Justice, in the phenomenological approach, is "an anthropological form of
coexistence," a coexistence which demands for its actu-
alization that "collective subjects speak a minimum 'yes'
to one another." That minimum "yes," whose boundaries
may shift with the actual conditions and relationships
about which positive sciences enlighten us, is the natural
law phenomenologically construed. There is nothing inevitable about such a law—it requires the implementation of human subjects who create the history of the
world. But it does offer more, according to its advocates,
"than an emotional form of powerlessness" as a defense
against the endless manipulation of life upon this
planet.[62]

It is true that the tendency in Catholicism, especially
since the Second Vatican Council, is to base ethical evaluations upon a more obviously biblical anthropology, but
a faith-inspired ethic was never intended to exclude the
proper function of one philosophically based.[63] The use
by John Paul of Genesis is an excellent example of how the
two can be worked together. The human person bears
the divine image in a significant way because of his/her
gifts of intelligence and freedom which are to be used
responsibly. In this sense, an ethic based upon rational
principles is not really foreign to a biblical view of the
world, is not "unevangelical," as is sometimes asserted.

New reworkings of natural law outside a religious
context seek to address what is an even more urgent task
today, "human responsibility in a causally determinate
natural order."[64] An objectively valid moral order, ultimately, is our only defense against those who would
determine for us the value of a life. In his grim book, *The
Nazi Doctors: Medical Killing and the Psychology of Gen-*

ocide, Robert Jay Lifton argues that the killing of persons regarded as "unworthy of life" was not a mere practical necessity in the waging of a war but was what the war itself was all about.[65]

The prayer for wisdom by Solomon is really the plea of all generations not merely to follow their own selfish paths but to discover the intentions and ways of God as we share in his governance of the world:

> God of our ancestors, Lord of mercy, who by your word have made the universe, and in your wisdom have fitted human beings to rule the creatures that you have made, to govern the world in holiness and saving justice and in honesty of soul to dispense fair judgment, grant me Wisdom, consort of your throne, and do not reject me from the number of your children. For I am your servant, son of your serving maid, a feeble man, with little time to live, with small understanding of justice and the laws.[66]

Both Marxist collectivism and liberal capitalism profess themselves to be "scientific," observant of "laws" that they supposedly have discovered. In fact of such "laws," spiritual values such as those in the Book of Genesis are regarded as "matters of sentiment, high culture and religion, with no relevance for our day-to-day behavior. Values do not interfere with the economic laws."[67] John Paul feels obliged to oppose both ideologies. In doing so he is not defending "spiritual life" taken thus as an abstraction, but rather life itself in all its dimensions.

The surprise and the rejection from some quarters

regarding the encyclical missed how traditional John Paul's teaching was. It also manifested profound cynicism. One critique in the pages of the *New York Times* called the pope naive to think there are today "persons of good will" to whom he could speak on both sides of the ongoing ideological conflict. Pope John Paul in so speaking was making a faith statement, a faith in what Genesis declares with equal courage: that even in a world of sin "there exist in the human person sufficient qualities and energies, a fundamental 'goodness' (Gn 1:31), because we are the image of our Creator, placed under the redemptive influence of Christ who united himself in some way with every person and because the effective action of the Holy Spirit 'fills the earth' " (Wis 1:7). 68

Paul VI spoke of the church as an "expert in humanity" and as such having a competence to speak on questions relating to human life. Drawing upon the wisdom found in Genesis and the other resources of her tradition that are expanding her vision to include not just humanity but the earth humanity inhabits, the church may perhaps one day feel she has the right to call herself also expert in life on earth.

Maybe the freshness of vision about life on earth which Genesis manifests is akin to the first glimpses of the earth from outer space which is one of the privileged experiences of our time. John Paul II referred to it in his New Year's message of 1987:

> From the time that we were first able to see pictures of the world from space, a perceptible change has taken place in our understanding of our planet, and of its immense beauty and fragility.69

The astronaut Michael Collins confirms this impression: "When I traveled to the moon," he writes, "it wasn't my proximity to that battered rockpile I remember so vividly, but rather what I saw when I looked back at my fragile home—a glistening, inviting beacon, delicate blue and white, a tiny outpost suspended in the black infinity. Earth is to be treasured and nurtured, something precious that *must* endure."[70]

Both pope and astronaut use the word "fragile" in describing our earth home. It is an adjective that arouses spontaneous feelings of protectiveness and caring. Perhaps this is the feeling that prompts John Paul whenever he arrives for a pastoral visit to a distant place to bend to the ground and kiss the earth before shaking any human hand.

6 HUMILITAS

An important element in biblical revelation is that we are "only strangers and nomads on earth . . . in search of a homeland, one that is heavenly."[1] As a "chosen race, a priestly kingdom, a holy nation, a people of God," we are to live a kind of nomadic life and keep ourselves "free from the contamination of this world until we arrive at our goal, the salvation of our souls."[2] Our hope is for an end to this world of tears and of death and for the coming down from heaven of a new Jerusalem, a new heaven and a new earth,[3] as John envisioned it in the Bible's final book, echoing Third Isaiah:

> Look, here God lives among human beings. He will make his home among them; they will be his people and he will be their God, God-with-them. He will wipe away all tears from their eyes; there will be no more death, and no more mourning of sadness or pain. The world of the past has gone.[4]

The experience of alienation from our surroundings, so characteristic of Israel in exile and the church in a time of persecution, is also a hallmark of modernity. Nowhere is this more apparent than in the life and writings of one of the prophetic voices of the early twentieth century, Franz Kafka, in whom feelings of estrangement were accompanied, as they are in persons of a religious sensibility, with the hope for a "promised land." In the case of Kafka, the "promised land" was very concretely construed.

What we wish to note in this final chapter is that the guiding image of the "promised land" is not put forth as a cosmic myth but as the very future of this earth. Its coming down from heaven is not to be taken, as it often is, as a sign of its cosmic and mythological meaning removed from the earth, but an attestation of the fact that the "new heavens and the new earth" will come primarily from divine redemption, joined to the human efforts and the human hope that it inspires.

After discussing "the search for a home" and its arrival-point, the "land of promise," we will conclude with some basic elements for a household code for our life on earth. Such "house rules" (*Haustafeln*, the German exegetes called them) from the secular culture found their way into both Testaments which adapted them according to their own particular viewpoints. It is appropriate to speak of such "house rules" if we take seriously our continued life on earth and if we look to a final accommodation of divine revelation and human wisdom. Ecology, literally "the science of the home," is appropriate activity for those who truly feel the earth to be home, at least in hope and promise.

THE SEARCH FOR A HOME

Franz Kafka (1883–1924), in a telling passage from a letter to a friend, wrote, "I like hotel rooms. I always feel immediately at home in hotel rooms, more so than at home."[5] This "Kafkaesque" vision of modern life as an extended stay in a hotel, which ironically has a greater feel of home than home itself, turned out to be a strikingly accurate premonition of the evils and collapsed certitudes of the world as it moved into the economic, political, and social upheavals that were soon to ensue. Freed from the ghetto, the first generation of acculturated Jews to which Kafka's father belonged were exposed in a more direct way to anti-Semitism and a search for identity in their new urban exile. In the case of the father, identity was achieved by the accumulation of wealth through meaningless labor—an identity Kafka vehemently rejected.

"This was the atmosphere of Kafka's world," his biographer writes, "dense with hate. But he had never known any other, and it took time for him to understand why he had trouble breathing. Understanding, when it came, turned out to be as toxic as the air itself."[6] The opening sentence of Kafka's novel *The Trial*, the story of a respectable bank clerk who suddenly is arrested and spends the rest of his life trying to find out the charge against him, carries an ominousness that was prophetic: "Someone must have maligned Joseph K, for without having done anything wrong, he was arrested one morning."[7]

It is even more telling that Kafka found his existence so hotel-like when you realize that except for the last nine months of his life he never really left his parents' home in Prague. "What he had taken for the world," his biographer comments, "turned out to be no more than a fenced-in patch of backyard at the end of the wilderness—a vast silence."[8] It was not the frightening silence of outer space as experienced by Pascal, but something of still greater spiritual significance, a vast emptiness on the earth itself, in the center of the human heart.

In a letter to a friend Kafka tried to explain the nature of this pervasive unease:

> You say, Milena, that you can't understand it. Try to understand it by calling it an illness. It is one of the many manifestations of illness which psychoanalysis prides itself on having uncovered. I don't call it illness, I regard the therapeutic application of psychoanalysis as a hopeless error. All these ostensible illnesses, sad as they may seem, are matters of faith, the efforts of a human being in distress to sink roots into some maternal soil. Thus psychoanalysis also perceives the origin of religion as nothing more than what, in its view, also causes the "illnesses" of the individual. . . . Such roots, however, sunk into real soil, are not after all, humanity's individual and interchangeable property but preformed in his nature.[9]

The final phase of Kafka's life was given over to a fantasy about returning to Palestine. He, the self-described unbelieving, nonobservant but "repentent" Jew, wanted desperately to emigrate to Canaan, the Promised Land, the place of miracle and hope after all human rescue efforts had failed. He would be the waiter and his friend Dora would be the cook in a restaurant they would open in Tel Aviv: "Canaan is perforce my only

Promised Land, for no third place exists for humankind," reads one of Kafka's entries in his diary.[10] By this, a commentator writes, Kakfa means that "the purely spiritual world detached from the physical, is not an inhabitable place. Kafka was no Buddhist and did not stop at some kind of Nirvana as though having reached some absolute end. . . . There are only two, not three, possible dwelling places: the world of this life and the world of perfect restoration of all life at the end of this world and the beginning of the other. Canaan, the land promised to Israel, was Kafka's only Promised Land."[11]

To the human search for a home in this land of estrangement the divine answer comes in the form of the land of promise. It is a divine answer to a profound human longing, but as the case of Kafka demonstrates, the place where the promise is fulfilled is not in the mind or in the cosmos but must somehow involve the earth if it is to be a true home of humans whose name is Adam, "the one taken from the earth."

THE LAND OF PROMISE

"A Jew dying far away might ask for a few grains of Jerusalem earth to be sprinkled on his coffin, and some people went to their graves with twigs tied into their hands that might take root and grow the other way."[12] So writes Eleanor Munro in her "pilgrim's book about pilgrimage," *On Glory Roads*. It is a heartfelt book describing pilgrimages to the sacred places of four world religions prompted by the author's sense of loss at her father's death. That death was even more poignant because the father was an atheist, "a true son of the Enlightenment," committed to the scientific method. "But his atheism had hedged him in," the author decided, looking back. "Where is my father now?" she asks herself at each sacred place, seeking to be not a mere observer or tourist but a genuine pilgrim. "I am nothing," she must admit, and in the end, after experiencing in all their vividness the rituals of Hinduism, Buddhism, Judaism, and Christianity, she concludes that they all are the geometry of the mind expressing the human desire to *survive* in the cosmos if no longer upon the earth.

We need a new myth, she concludes, not a cosmic one like the old ones, but one "more generous," one that shows the earth itself "counts for something," "the only sacred space where pilgrimage can now unfold," this "small blue-green floating spore across whose surface an edge of sunlight races, right to left."[13]

What Munro the pilgrim misses is that the Land of Promise for those who believe is the future of a place familiar to them, a place where God has been revealed. It is a place on earth. In fact she takes note of such a place at the very start of her disappointing pilgrimages to strange and foreign lands. With surer instinct, after her father's death, she feels compelled to take her sons to the Hebrides, the land of her Highland-descended father. "I wanted to show my sons the country [that was] theirs."[14]

"The universe gives me the creeps," she quotes Willem de Kooning as saying.[15] Of course it does, because the earth and not the universe is our home, and not just any part of the earth but precisely that part where we have sunk our roots.

Annie Dillard, author of *Pilgrim at Tinker Creek*, after several books of spiritual pilgrimage, has written a finely observed reminiscence of growing up in Pittsburgh. She

begins: "When everything else has gone from my brain—
the President's name, the state capitals, the neigh-
borhoods where I lived, and then my own name and
what it was on earth I sought, and then at length the
faces of my friends, and finally the faces of my family—
when all this has dissolved, what will be left, I believe, is
topology: the dreaming memory of land as it lay this way
and that."[16]

What the Christian religion tells Dillard is that life is
not a Platonic dream.[17] "A dream," in fact, she concludes, "consists of little more than its setting. . . . For it
is not you or I that is important, neither what sort we
might be nor how we came to be each where we are.
What is important is anyone's coming awake and discovering a place . . . our present world."[18] But you have
to take it on faith, she says, that these various and dis-
crete people and places and things of your life cohere,
that they are part of one world, "that you didn't drop
chopped from house to house, coast to coast, life to
life."[19]

In an earlier book Dillard notes that the Israelites had
to be warned from frequenting sacred groves; "I wish I
could find one," she quips. "We as a people have moved
from pantheism to pan-atheism," she continues, and
then intuits the reason: "We live where we want to
live."[20] The sacred grove is nowhere to be found in a
mobile society, one that is uncannily like the peoples in
Genesis who did not live in their assigned places and
instead attempted to build a tower to the sky.[21]

Walter Bruegemann has pointed out the impoverish-
ment of presenting the biblical revelation "as though
these events which happened between Yahweh and his
people could have happened anywhere." The problem

the Bible addresses, according to him, "is the central human problem of homelessness" and it does so by giving us rootage in the Promised Land.[22] The Messiah, the stranger and alien one who "has no place to lay his head," comes to assign each of us our place in the kingdom of his Father.[23]

Certainly this essential point was missed with disastrous personal consequences by Simone Weil (1909–43), like Kafka another seminal writer of our century. Also a nonobservant Jew, Weil felt impelled to embrace Christ but could not become a member of the church. Perhaps what held her back was her Platonism, a Platonism which made her disdain all traces of Judaism in Christianity. Her biographer concludes she was a Gnostic, and Gnosticism was that heresy which "issued out of Christianity and was an attempt to develop its Hellenic element by diminishing the element of Judaism that it conserved."[24] Weil mysteriously starved herself to death living in exile in England while World War II raged.

Weil saw the "essential point" of Christianity and of Platonism to be the same: "It is only the thought of perfection that produces any good." The entire universe is "nothing but a great metaphor. God is the sole good. He has the monopoly of good. God is outside this world."[25] A similar denial of the world is found in the Buddhism that for Munro was such a dead end: "Life is a journey, the universe an inn."[26]

How far these sentiments are from Genesis and its courageous faith-statement about the world, a statement that cannot be verified apart from faith because it is certainly different from the world that we presently experience, "And God found it to be very good." Hope in the Promised Land and in the restoration and redemption of the creation concludes the biblical story just as Genesis begins it.[27] An essential part of that conclusion for Christians is the belief in the resurrection of the body, a doctrine that was so offensive to Greek culture.[28] Belief in the resurrection is grounded in the resurrection of Christ himself from the dead, the "first fruits"[29] of those that sleep. The New Testament narratives insist that the resurrected Jesus, though he lives now in a new form, is identical with the Jesus who died upon the cross. In a similar way it is our bodily existence that will be raised, not just some "spiritual" part of us that is presumed to be endowed by nature with immortality. Both Judaism and Christianity agree that there is only One who is by nature immortal, the Blessed One, blessed be he!

The "new" heavens and the "new" earth are genuinely new and not merely the continuation of life as we now know it. "Behold, I am doing something new," says the Lord.[30] Unlike the ancient Egyptians who in their desire to give the Pharaoh immortality provisioned him with a mummified body and food and wealth for his continued existence, St. Paul asserts that there is an amazing transformation of the present life into something we cannot even imagine or conceive: It is like the difference, he says, between a lowly seed put into the ground and the full-grown plant.[31]

It was this radical newness that the traditionalist Sadducees missed when they tried to demonstrate the absurd complexities that would ensue should the dead arise; they cited to Jesus the case of a women who successively married seven brothers and asked, "At the resurrection, whose wife among the seven will she be, since she had been married to them all?" Jesus responds by asserting that present earthly arrangements do not pertain: "You are wrong because you understand neither the scriptures nor the power of God. For at the resurrection men and women do not marry; no, they are like the angels in heaven."[32]

It is the outpouring of the Holy Spirit upon the earth that is the true result of the life, death, and resurrection of Jesus, the Spirit of life, the Spirit who is the "downpayment"[33] of the life to come and the source of our hope.

In a world subject to obvious corruption everywhere—according to some, in the grip of an ineluctable fate and to others, the victim of human sin and selfishness—hope comes as a precious and dazzling gift. It is not based upon optimistic assessments of our human prospects scientifically or statistically calculated; neither does it arise out of a mystical belief in the evolution of some natural process: Christian hope is in the power of God to save. Such hope is the hallmark of being a Christian. "The essential characteristic of Christian Antiquity," a patristics scholar has written, "is its optimistic certitude about salvation, a confidence that is all the more tranquil the closer one gets to its origins. Jesus came to bring salvation; it is enough to believe in him and to be baptized to be saved."[34] The first Christian martyrs went to their deaths in the Roman Colosseum *singing*.

The biblical hope for the future as contained in the image of the land of promise was for the hope of Israel as a people and not merely for the salvation of individuals. It is furthermore a salvation in which all the peoples of the world will share. "My house will be called a house of prayer for all peoples," Jesus declares in Mark,[35] recalling the words of Third Isaiah.[36] Commentators who have noted correctly the historical connection between religion and devotion to the land have sometimes emphasized only the negative aspects of such devotion as these express themselves in nationalistic exclusivism and religious warfare while missing the point that devotion to a place on earth need not preclude a genuine universalism. In fact, it may be the only real possibility for such universalism, for how can we be inspired by statistics about no place in particular?

Conor Cruise O'Brien has written extensively about places of religious conflict in our day, notably the Middle East and Northern Ireland. In his lectures collected together under the title *God Land*, O'Brien seeks to draw the connection between belief that "God chose a particular people and promised them a particular land" and the pernicious nationalisms that have plagued our life on earth. Sometimes that nationalism is explicitly religious, such as O'Brien finds in the Old Testament; in other, more secular times, virulent nationalism arises as a God substitute. In this regard, O'Brien gives Jesus and Paul high marks for supposedly removing the Promised Land from this earth entirely:

> The Old Testament, interpreted in a Christian sense, remains of divine inspiration. But the combination of religion with nationalism, which appears so clearly in the Old Testament, disappears in the New. The early Christians allegorized the Old Testament right out of this world and into the next. The Promised Land, which the Patriarchs took to be Canaan, turns out to be Heaven. The early Christians, as well as spiritualizing the Old Testament, also internationalize it. The *real* Chosen People are no longer the Jews but all those—of whatever language, culture, or nation—who know themselves to be re-

deemed by Christ's sacrifice on the Cross. That is the new Covenant, which the older covenants are to prefigure.[37]

Even in the modern world, O'Brien quotes a Jewish authority as saying that Judaism is an earthy religion. "The earthiness is part of its power, and the promise of the Land is part of the earthiness." "The early Christians tried to get rid of the earthiness," O'Brien adds, "believing that the earth itself was, in any case, about to end. But the earth stayed where it was, more or less, and many of the Christians came back to earth."[38]

We would say in response that there is no contradiction between earthiness and spirituality, and there is no necessary connection between the notion of the Promised Land and imperialistic nationalism. O'Brien as a self-professed agnostic no doubt conceives the heavenly and the supernatural as having no real connection with the earth, but he also misses one of the most original aspects of the Old Testament, namely that while every nation is given its land to dwell upon by God, Israel's possession of its assigned land is made conditional. You may have this land, God says, only if you are moral; Israel's possession is thus made dependent upon righteous behavior. Such an ethical conception of the relationship to land surely takes us beyond mere nationalism into another order of things.[39]

Armed with hope, we are given the incentive to advance God's purposes in the world and to hasten his coming reign. It is not as if our efforts by themselves will transform the world, but we are convinced that in God's kingdom "we will find our efforts once again, cleansed

this time from sin and illumined and transfigured."[40]
The church's still-developing social doctrine is a sign of
the religious commitment to this world and its fate. For
the Greeks, who in this case would be in agreement with
Christianity, the nonparticipants in the life of "the City"
were *idioi* ("idiots"—people who are on their own). A
Christian would apply the same term to those who ab-
stain, even for so-called religious reasons, from civic life
today.[41]

"Secularity," in fact, is the dominant characteristic of
the life of the baptized members of the church. They are
to work out their salvation, according to the Second
Vatican Council, not only by active participation in the
life of the church but also by their proficiency in secular
affairs.[42] The clergy, though set apart "as witnesses and
dispensers of a life other than that of this earth,"[43] also
have a role to play as educators of conscience.

Whitehead's famous dictum, "Nothing perishes,"
thus is given theological justification in the unshakable
hope that "all that can be destroyed can be brought back
to life,"[44] for "God is the God of the living and not of the
dead."[45] It is God himself and alone, the origin and goal
of our life, whose home we believe the earth will become
once again, who is the object of our hope and desire, as
we look forward to the day when God will be "all in all,"
"everything to everyone."[46]

A HOUSEHOLD CODE

On the ladder of virtues, faith, hope, and love are at
the very top, the three "theological" virtues that have
their origin in God. The very bottom rung is humility. It's

not much, as they say, but it is a beginning and has all the importance of a beginning, just as, according to Arendt, Christianity vastly increased the importance of this world and of existence, and activity in this world is the irreplaceable beginning place of the next world.[47]

The root meaning of humility is "humus," earth or soil. The humble have their feet planted firmly upon the ground and at the same time, recognizing their own earthliness and limitedness, perceive divine gifts truly as divine gifts and the ladder-link between the earth and God. Just as Jacob in Genesis took a rock for a pillow and dreamt of a ladder "that rested upon the ground with its top reaching to heaven," so the humble awaking from humanity's sleep can realize, "Truly the Lord is in this place and I did not know it. . . . This is no other than the house of God, this is the gate of heaven."[48] Jesus will later rebuild the ladder between earth and heaven.[49] At his death it is said the veil of the Temple was shorn in two,[50] for God is no longer hidden but walks the earth once more. Jesus at his resurrection at first is mistaken for the gardener, tilling his new Eden.[51] The earth has become God's house again.

"Small is beautiful," E. F. Schumacher said, speaking humbly. Humility respects the human scale of things, eschews overweening ambition, does not build towers in Babel nor embark upon social engineering that gets out of hand and ends up in a Holocaust. It works with mustard seeds and is satisfied to await the results.

Humility's neighbors at the bottom of the ladder are modesty, prudence, and temperance, virtues for the wait until the appearance of our blessed hope.[52] They are the kin of poverty of spirit and meekness, the meekness of those who will "inherit the land."[53] Together these humble virtues are a way to live upon the earth without harming anything. The ladder of virtue is not a scale of beings from "lowest to highest"; on the contrary, it is a way for all to live together in harmony.

The sun and the moon are not seen by the humble as alien spheres but as "brother" and "sister." It is not their silence and their eternity that impress themselves upon us, but their affinity to us and their benevolence. The ravaging wolf of Gubbio was tamed when Francis loved it; nature rises up and rebels only when it is not loved.

Though we are born of the earth, we are not born humble. Humility must be cultivated as Adam was instructed to cultivate the earth. Humility makes us delight in the place where we live, makes us happy to be in our skins. It makes us feel finally "at home." But the way of humility is not an easy one, especially for modern persons. We have a highly developed sense of our individuality and greatly underdeveloped sense of our peoplehood.

I recall having a tour of the lower regions of the great Basilica of St. Peter built at the dawning of the modern era by an unrepeatable constellation of great artists. Begun in 1506, St. Peter's was formally consecrated 120 years later. It still strikes us as a "modern" building, self-consciously the "largest" church in the world with markers upon its pavements of the comparative sizes of other churches around the world, all falling short of its enormity. My guide for this tour was a cherished friend, then nearing his ninth decade of life. For many of those years Count Enrico Galeazzi (1896–1986) had served as architect of the basilica, advising on its continuous changes and improvements. We entered a vast underground space closed to the public. There lying on their sides were huge granite columns which he identified as belonging to the Constantinian basilica, the first upon this site. The columns in the semidarkness resembled fallen trees from a giant forest. The first explorations beneath the floor of the original shrine took place when the new basilica was rising. A hole in an ancient mosaic ceiling of a tomb which depicts Apollo Helios was made at that time, but Raphael, Sangello, Bernini, Michelangelo, and Bramante, the Count explained, had no real antiquarian interest. There was no great desire to explore the past. This was "their" moment to make their mark upon history. While the ancient iconographers fasted and prayed as they painted the divine face, scrupulously following venerable traditions of depiction and never daring to add their names as the authors of these works, which were not considered so much as personal creations but as divine communications—the Renaissance artists saw no need to remain anonymous, writing their signatures across all they created. The desire was to create something new, different, individual.

The author of the First Letter of Peter addressed his disparate flock and told them "once you were no people, but now you have become the people of God."[54] They were "no people" because they did not form one ethnic group as did Judaism of old. We moderns, or postmoderns, are "no people" for other reasons as well. In our greed, individualism and selfishness, we, like the epistle's "no people," have a need, an even more urgent one, to acquire the virtues it regards as hallmarks of the Christian life: "brotherly and sisterly affection, kindness and humblemindedness."[55] The letter concludes, "Above all, keep your love for one another at full strength. . . . Be hospitable to one another without complaining. What-

ever gift each of you may have received, use it in service
to one another, like good stewards dispensing the grace of
God in its varied forms. . . . Indeed, all of you should
wrap yourselves in the garment of humility towards each
other because God sets his face against the arrogant but
favors the humble."[56]

How exotic this catalog of virtues. Yet they comprise
not just a survival kit for continued life upon the earth.
They are the first lights of the dawning kingdom of God.

* * *

After we had finished our tour of St. Peter's, my guide
made a personal comment, one that was all the more
striking because it expressed a simpler faith than his
cosmopolitan exterior might suggest: "I have never
ceased to be astonished," this papal advisor reflected,
"that for three hundred years after the death of St. Peter
there was nothing on this site." Nothing but occasional
Christians coming to a tomb in the middle of a pagan
cemetery and lowering pieces of clothing down a channel
to touch the holy bones of the apostle, in the hope that
they like all the earth will be stirred to life again at the
glorious resurrection.

Notes

Citations from the documents of Vatican II are from *Vatican Council II: The Conciliar and Post Conciliar Documents*, edited by Austin Flannery (Northport, NY: Costello, 1984).

Preface

1. E. F. Schumacher, *Small Is Beautiful: Economics as if People Mattered* (New York: Harper and Row, 1973). Schumacher later made explicit, for a modern audience presumably unacquainted with it, the connection with Christian philosophical tradition in his book *A Guide for the Perplexed* (New York: Harper and Row, 1977).

2. In 1986, at the invitation of Pope John Paul II, representatives of the world's major religions gathered in Assisi for a World Day of Prayer for Peace. In the same year, and at the same place, the World Wide Fund for Nature sponsored a conference of the world's religions.

The World Day of Prayer was held on October 27 and was a unique event of great symbolic value. Because of the diversity of conceptions regarding the divinity among the participants, they assembled, according to a formulation proposed by the pope, to "be together to pray," but not "to pray together": that is to say, each could pray according to the traditions of each, without having to water down their prayer expressions to accommodate all. Besides prayer, fasting and mutual hospitality were major elements.

The Fund for Nature similarly learned that a unified statement on religion and ecology was impossible. Instead, each religion offered its own perspective on how humanity and nature relate to one another, and these were incorporated into "The Assisi Declarations." Images of human stewardship for the creation were characteristic of Christianity, Judaism, and Islam. Hindus and Buddhists stressed the spiritual quality of all creation, a quality which humanity also shares but does not exclusively lay title to. For all religions, the issue of the environment was preeminently a spiritual issue more than anything else. See Joseph W. Meeker, "The Assisi Connection," *Wilderness*, Spring 1988, 61–63.

3. John Macquarrie, *The Humility of God* (Philadelphia: Westminster Press, 1978), 3–4.

4. Phlm 2:6; Col 1:19.

5. *Gaudium et spes*, no. 37.

6. Quoted by William James in *The Varieties of Religious Experience* (New York: Penguin Books, 1982), 41.

7. Lester Thurow, *The Zero-Sum Society* (New York: Basic Books, 1980), 105.

8. Peter Borrelli, "Epiphany: Religion, Ethics and the Environment," *The Amicus Journal*, Winter 1986, 34–41.

9. Hannah Arendt, *The Human Condition* (Chicago: University of Chicago Press, 1958), 2.

10. Ibid., 247.

Introduction

1. Paul and Anne Ehrlich, *Extinction: The Causes and Consequences of the Disappearance of Species* (New York: Ballantine Books, 1981), 58.

2. Aldo Leopold, *A Sand County Almanac* (New York: Ballantine Books, 1970), 237f.

3. St. Augustine, *Confessions*, bk. 7.

4. Heb 13:14.

5. G. L. Prestige in his classic work, *God in Patristic Thought* (London: SPCK, 1952), says the same thing: "Ideas were certainly adopted from pagan sources in the different efforts made to give a Christian explanation. But I do not think that any one such idea was ever imported without undergoing substantial modification to suit its new environment. The idea was cut to fit the Christian faith, not the faith trimmed to square with the imported conception" (xiii–xiv).

Cardinal Joseph Ratzinger, in his book *Eschatology: Death and Eternal Life* (Washington, DC: Catholic University of America Press, 1988; vol. 9 in the series Dogmatic Theology which he edited with Johann Auer), comments that when Matthew speaks of the "kingdom of heaven" he "is not concerned, any more than are Mark and Luke, with something

which is primarily in the world beyond. . . . First
and foremost Jesus is speaking not of a heavenly
reality but of something God is doing and will do in
the future here on earth" (5). Ratzinger cites the
appeal "save your soul" as an example of how in
modern times Christianity "has been reduced to the
level of individual persons, to the detriment of what
was once the core of both eschatology and the Christian message itself: the confident, corporate hope for
the imminent salvation of all the world" (26). After a
lifetime of teaching eschatology and initially attempting to do so in a "de-Platonized" manner,
Ratzinger contends a completely "de-Platonized" eschatology leaves out elements that the Christian tradition has found to be essential, notably personal
survival after death and the immortality of the soul.
Such an immortality, however, would not be that of
an independent principle, but, in the Christian
scheme, would have to be God conferred.

6. Mt 6:28.

7. Ps 145.

8. Ps 19.

9. National Conference of Catholic Bishops, *Economic
Justice for All: Pastoral Letter on Catholic Social
Teaching and the U.S. Economy* (Washington, DC:
United States Catholic Conference, 1986), no. 216.

10. Ibid., no. 12.

11. Barbara Ward, *A New Creation? Reflections on the
Environmental Issue* (Vatican City: Pontifical Commission Justitia et Pax, 1973), 17. This is volume 5 in
a series published to apply the teachings of the 1971
World Synod of Bishops regarding the relationship of

the Gospel and the work for justice. Ward was a synod consulter. On specifically economic issues, Ward wrote *Progress for a Small Planet* (New York: W. W. Norton, 1979).

12. J. B. Wiesner and H. F. York, *Scientific American* 211, no. 4 (1964): 26.

13. Garrett Hardin, "The Tragedy of the Commons," *Science* 162 (13 December 1968): 1245.

14. Daniel C. Maguire, *A New American Justice* (Minneapolis: Winston Press, 1980), 85–98.

15. Pope Paul VI, *Humanae vitae* ("On Human Life," 25 July 1968), no. 13.

16. Ibid., no. 16.

17. Ibid., no. 17.

18. Wendell Berry, "The Body and the Earth," *Recollected Essays, 1965–1980* (San Francisco: North Point Press, 1981), 304–5.

19. 1 Cor 7:31.

20. *Gaudium et spes*, no. 37.

21. Jn 17:9.

22. Pope John Paul II, *Christifideles laici* ("Apostolic Exhortation on the Laity," 30 December 1988), no. 27.

23. Jn 3:16.

24. See Joseph Sittler, *Essays on Nature and Grace* (Philadelphia: Fortress Press, 1972), 120.

25. *Gaudium et spes*, no. 57.

26. *Lumen gentium*, no. 48.

27. *Gaudium et spes*, no. 34.

28. See A. G. Mojtabai, *Blessed Assurance: At Home with*

the Bomb in Amarillo, Texas (Boston: Houghton Mifflin, 1986). See also Hal Lindsay, *The Late Great Planet Earth* (New York: Bantam Books, 1973).

29. *New York Times*, 21 June 1987, Arts and Leisure Section.

30. Karl Rahner, S. J., *Foundations of Christian Faith* (New York: Seabury Press, 1978), 151–52. But Rahner also may be cited as an example of how Christian appreciation of the salvation of the world is still in a state of development. Rahner defines the human person as "spirit-in-the-world," with emphasis on "spirit," the center of subjectivity and transcendence. Because the human person in this definition is not merely "spirit" but "spirit-in-the-world," Rahner concludes that the material world, our connatural environment, has to share in some way in our eternal fulfillment. It is thus in this roundabout way that Rahner can understand the salvation of the world. See Leo J. O'Donovan, S. J., ed., *A World of Grace* (New York: Seabury Press, 1980), 162.

31. Jn 4:23–24.

32. See Anscar J. Chupungco, O.S.B., *Cultural Adaptation of the Liturgy* (New York: Paulist Press, 1982), 18.

33. Eric Voegelin, "The Gospel and Culture," in *Jesus and Man's Hope*, vol. 2, ed. Donald G. Miller and Dikran Y. Hadidian (Pittsburgh Theological Seminary, 1971), 100–101.

34. Ibid., 61, 70.

35. Mt 13:44.

36. *Gaudium et spes*, no. 43.

37. See Charles M. Murphy, "Action for Justice as Con-

stitutive of the Preaching of the Gospel: What Did the 1971 Synod Mean?," in *Readings in Moral Theology,* vol. 5, ed. Charles E. Curran and Richard A. McCormick, S.J. (New York: Paulist Press, 1986), 150–66.

38. Harold J. Berman, *Law and Revolution: The Formation of the Western Legal Tradition* (Cambridge: Harvard University Press, 1983), 28.

39. See Paul Steidl-Meier, S. J., *Social Justice Ministry: Foundations and Concerns* (New York: Le Jacq, 1984), 3–24.

40. *Gaudium et spes,* no. 40.

41. Marcellino Zalba, S. J., *Theologiae moralis summa,* vol. 2 (Madrid: Biblioteca de Autures Cristianos, 1957), 296.

42. Ingrid Newkirk et al., "Just Like Us? Toward a Notion of Animal Rights," *Harper's,* August 1988, 43–52.

43. Mircea Eliade, *The Sacred and the Profane: The Nature of Religion,* trans. Willard R. Trask (New York: Harcourt, Brace and World, 1959), 116.

44. Ibid., 179.

45. Paul Tillich, *The Shaking of the Foundations* (New York: Charles Scribner's Sons, 1948), 86. See also his chapter, "Nature and Sacrament," in *The Protestant Era* (Chicago: University of Chicago Press, 1984), 94–112.

46. Marguerite Yourcenar, *With Open Eyes* (Boston: Beacon Press, 1984), 23–24.

47. G. K. Chesterton, "The Concrete and the Abstract," in *The Man Who Was Orthodox: A Selection of the Uncollected Writings of G. K. Chesterton,* arranged and

introduced by A. L. Maycock (London: Dennis Dobson, 1963), 179.

48. See Rudolf Otto, *The Idea of the Holy* (New York: Oxford University Press, 1968), 25–40. See also John Macquarrie's critique of Otto in *In Search of Humanity* (New York: Crossroad, 1985), 199–221.

49. Anne Morrow Lindbergh, *Gift from the Sea* (New York: Vintage Books, 1978), 128.

Chapter 1: The Environmental Movement

1. David Vogel, "A Big Agenda," *Wilson Quarterly*, Autumn 1987, 51.

2. Walker Percy, *The Thanatos Syndrome* (New York: Farrar, Straus and Giroux, 1987), 333.

3. John Muir, *The Yosemite* (San Francisco: Sierra Club, 1988), 192–93.

4. Aldo Leopold, *A Sand County Almanac* (New York: Ballantine Books, 1970), 239.

5. Ibid., 238.

6. Ibid., 246.

7. Ibid., 47.

8. Charles E. Little, "Letting Leopold Down," *Wilderness*, Summer 1987, 47.

9. *Gaudium et spes*, no. 69.

10. Rachel Carson, *Silent Spring* (Boston: Houghton Mifflin, 1962), pp. 8–9.

11. See William Tucker, *Progress and Privilege: America in the Age of Environmentalism* (New York: Anchor/Doubleday, 1982).

12. Ehrlich and Ehrlich, *Extinction*, 263 (Introduction, note 1, above).

13. *New York Times*, 25 September 1986, Section A.

14. Ehrlich and Ehrlich, *Extinction*, 61.

15. Peter Borelli, "Epiphany, Religion, Ethics and the Bible," *The Amicus Journal*, Winter 1986, 37.

Chap. 2: Home or Hotel: An Ethic for the Earth

1. Edward O. Wilson, *On Human Nature* (Cambridge: Harvard University Press, 1978), 195.

2. Ibid., 167.

3. Ibid., 71.

4. Ibid., 192.

5. See G. L. Prestige, *God in Patristic Thought*, xiii–xviii (Introduction, note 5, above).

6. Etienne Gilson, *The Philosopher and Theology* (New York: Random House, 1962), 9–12.

7. Eph 1:9–10. See Vatican Council I, the dogmatic constitution *Dei Filius*, chap. 4.

8. See Keith E. Yandell, "Protestant Theology and Natural Science in the Twentieth Century," in *God and Nature: Historical Essays on the Encounter between Christianity and Science*, ed. David C. Lindberg and Ronald L. Numbers (Berkeley: University of California Press, 1968), 461.

9. See Ernan McMullin, "Natural Science and Belief in a Creator," in *Religion, Science and the Search for Wisdom: Proceedings of a Conference on Religion and Science*, September 1986 (Washington, DC: Bishops'

Committee on Human Values, National Conference of Catholic Bishops, 1987), 16.

10. St. Augustine, Letter 120, *Corpus Scriptorum Ecclesiasticorum Latinorum*, vol. 34, ed. A. Goldbacher (Vienna: F. Tempsky, 1895), 705–7.

11. St. Augustine, *Enchiridion*, trans. Albert Outler, Library of Christian Classics (Philadelphia: Westminster Press, 1955), 342.

12. Lindberg and Numbers, *God and Nature*, 9.

13. Stephen W. Hawking, *A Brief History of Time* (New York: Bantam Books, 1988), 175.

14. Ibid., 116.

15. *L'Osservatore Romano*, Weekly Edition (English), 5 January 1981, 6.

16. Jeremy Bernstein, "Cosmology," *New Yorker*, 6 June 1988, 121.

17. Karl Rahner, S. J., "Natural Science and Reasonable Faith," *Theological Investigations*, vol. 21 (New York: Crossroad, 1988), 16–55.

18. The letter in English, dated 1 June 1988, appeared in *L'Osservatore Romano* for 26 October 1988, and was reprinted in *Origins* 18, no. 23 (17 November 1988): 376.

19. Ibid., 377.

20. Ibid., 378.

21. See Anne Lonergan and Caroline Richards, eds., *Thomas Berry and the New Cosmology* (Mystic, CT: Twenty-Third Publications, 1987).

22. Michael Walzer, *Interpretation and Social Criticism* (Cambridge: Harvard University Press, 1987), 17–22.

23. Northrope Frye, *The Great Code* (San Diego: Harcourt Brace Jovanovich, 1982), xii.

24. Ibid., xviii.

25. Harold Bloom, "Literature as the Bible," *New York Review of Books* 35, no. 5 (31 March 1988): 23–25. Walzer's *Exodus and Revolution* (New York: Basic Books, 1985) shows how the Book of Exodus has shaped Western political thought, especially with regard to the possibility of this world's redemption, liberation, and revolution. Walzer demonstrates that readers of Exodus have found not only a record of God's dealings with his people but a guide for the conceptualization of their lives.

26. Walzer, *Interpretation and Social Criticism*, 4.

27. Ibid., 6–8.

28. Ibid., 12.

29. Ibid., 16.

30. Ibid., 61. Along similar lines, see David Tracy, *Plurality and Ambiguity* (San Francisco: Harper and Row, 1987), chap. 1, "Interpretation, Conversation, Argument," 1–27.

31. Josef Fuchs, S. J., *Christian Morality: The Word Becomes Flesh* (Washington, DC: Georgetown University Press, 1987), 17.

32. Bernard Williams, *Ethics and the Limits of Philosophy* (Cambridge: Harvard University Press, 1985), vii.

33. Ibid., 18.

34. Ibid., 197.

35. Ibid., 201.

36. Fuchs, *Christian Morality*, 5.

37. Cynthia Ozick, "Sholem Aleichem's Revolution," *New Yorker*, 18 March 1988, 99.

38. Mk 1:15.

39. Wolfgang Schrage, *The Ethics of the New Testament*, trans. David E. Green (Philadelphia: Fortress Press, 1988), 3.

Chapter 3: The Silence of Space, The Eternity of Time

1. A large retrospective of the Hudson River School was mounted by the Metropolitan Museum of Art, New York City, October 1987–January 3, 1988.

   The case of the poet Emily Dickinson may be cited as an example of one whose poetic œuvre manifests the impact of the new scientific world-view upon a traditional religious sensibility. "All of America was falling away from the faith of the Fathers," writes her biographer. "The New Jerusalem was a faded memory to most, and the vigor of God's presence was leaving the land. Quite independently of the poet's challenge, words were losing the shadow of supernatural significance" (Cynthia Griffin Wolff, *Emily Dickinson* [New York: Alfred A. Knopf, 1986], 451). Dickinson could take no comfort from the higher reality espoused by the Transcendentalists; this was no substitute for the biblical God. Her poetry, nonetheless, was a "journey into faith" for, in the end, she discovers God within the course of everyday life. God in Jesus, Emily realized with awe, in apparent humility, had elected to become one of us. Wolff concludes, "Over and over again, the motif of 'the House' appears throughout this verse, but now Dickinson has become willing to accept the blissful expectation of this future estate without also possessing the certainty that could only come with seeing God on earth" (506).

2. Cited by Romano Guardini, *Pascal for Our Time* (New York: Herder and Herder, 1966), 59.

3. Lines from the Mémorial found on his person after his death. Guardini, *Pascal for Our Time*, 33–34.

4. Guardini, *Pascal*, 129.

5. Claude Cuénot, *Teilhard de Chardin* (Baltimore: Helicon Press, 1965), 211.

6. Cited by Henri de Lubac, S. J., *The Religion of Teilhard de Chardin* (New York: Descleies, 1967), 223.

7. Teilhard de Chardin, *The Divine Milieu* (New York: Harper and Row, 1960), 45.

8. Cited by Pierre Leroy, S. J., in his introduction to *The Divine Milieu*, 13.

9. 1 Cor 15:28.

10. De Lubac, *Teilhard de Chardin*, 155.

11. Pierre Teilhard de Chardin, *The Phenomenon of Man* (New York: Harper, 1959), 11.

12. De Lubac, *Teilhard de Chardin*, 212.

13. 1 Cor 15:47–48.

14. De Lubac, *Teilhard de Chardin*, 142.

15. A. R. Ammons, *Sumerian Vistas* (New York: W. W. Norton, 1988).

16. Helen Vendler, "Veracity Unshaken," *New Yorker*, 15 February 1988, 103.

17. *Gaudium et spes*, no. 4.

18. *Gaudium et spes*, no. 10, citing Col 1:15.

19. *Gaudium et spes*, nos. 23–32.

20. *Gaudium et spes*, no. 36.

21. De Chardin, *The Divine Milieu*, 56.

22. *Gaudium et spes*, no. 39.

23. Letter of Agostino Cardinal Casaroli, Vatican secretary of state, 12 May 1981, addressed to Paul Poupard, rector of the Institut Catholique, Paris.

24. John B. Cobb, Jr., *Process Theology as Political Theology* (Philadelphia: Westminster Press, 1982), xiii.

25. Johann Baptist Metz, *Faith in History and Society: Toward a Practical Fundamental Theology* (New York: Seabury Press, 1980), 73.

26. Lynn White, Jr., "The Historical Roots of Ecologic Crisis," *Science* 155 (10 March 1967): 1206.

27. Joseph Sittler, *Essays on Nature and Grace* (Philadelphia: Fortress Press, 1985).

28. Jürgen Moltmann, *The Crucified God*, trans. R. A. Wilson and John Bowden (San Francisco: Harper and Row, 1974), 332–35.

29. Jürgen Moltmann, *God in Creation: A New Theology of Creation and the Spirit of God* (San Francisco: Harper and Row, 1985), 59.

30. Ibid., 225.

31. Ibid., 226.

32. Charles Birch and John B. Cobb, Jr., *The Liberation of Life* (Cambridge: Cambridge University Press, 1981), 199.

33. Ibid., 158.

34. Charles Hartshorne, *The Divine Relativity: A Social*

Conception of God (New Haven: Yale University Press, 1948), 1–94.

35. Acts 17:28.

36. *Gaudium et spes*, no. 22.

37. John Paul II, *Salvifici doloris* ("Of Saving Suffering," 1984), no. 26.

38. Cobb, *Process Theology*, 141.

39. Gordon D. Kaufman, "A Problem for Theology: The Concept of Nature," *Harvard Theological Review* 65 (1972), 337–66.

40. Moltmann, *God in Creation*, 56.

41. Rom 1:20.

42. Cobb, *Process Theology*, 155.

43. *Gaudium et spes*, no. 22.

44. Mk 10:5.

Chapter 4: Genesis

1. See Richard J. Clifford, S. J., "Genesis 1–3: Permission to Exploit Nature?" *Bible Today* 26, no. 3 (May 1988): 133–37.

2. Gerhard von Rad, "The Theological Problem of the Old Testament Doctrine of Creation" in *The Problem of the Hexateuch and Other Essays*, trans. E. W. Trueman Dicken (New York: McGraw-Hill, 1966), 142.

3. Ps 104 and Gn 1 and 2 are examples of a separate emphasis upon creation itself apart from Israel.

4. Frank Moore Cross, *Canaanite Myth and Hebrew Epic: Essays in the History of the Religion of Israel* (Cambridge: Harvard University Press, 1973), 89.

Michael D. Coogan has studied in depth the continuities of Israel with Canaan. In his essay "Canaanite Origins and Lineage: Reflections on the Religion of Ancient Israel," he states provocatively: "The presupposition of this chapter is that for methodological purposes, it is essential to consider biblical religion as a subset of Canaanite religion. From a historical perspective it is more appropriate, then, to speak of the special development of the religion of ancient Israel, rather than of the ways in which it was influenced by other cultures, as though it was a static, fully formed reality subject only to tangential modification." The essay may be found in *Ancient Israelite Religion: Essays in Honor of Frank Moore Cross*, ed. P. D. Miller et al. (Philadelphia: Fortress Press, 1987), 115–24.

5. Ex 3:13–15.

6. Gn 1:26–31.

7. Bruce Vawter, *On Genesis: A New Reading* (Garden City, NY: Doubleday, 1977), 55.

8. John Macquarrie, *In Search of Deity: An Essay in Dialectical Theism* (New York: Crossroad, 1985), 64.

9. Ps 8:3–6.

10. John XXIII, *Mater et Magistra*, nos. 219–20.

11. Is 11:4–5; Lk 1:50–55, etc.

12. Gn 6:19.

13. Gn 9:9–17.

14. Gn 9:5.

15. Is 11:6.

16. Gn 1:20.

17. See Jn 34:11, 16; Zec 9:15, etc.

18. Dt 32:8–9.

19. Gn 11:4.

20. Gn 6:5.

21. See Richard J. Clifford, S. J., "The Hebrew Scriptures and the Theology of Creation," *Theological Studies* 46, no. 3 (September 1985): 509. To cite a New Testament example, at the death of Christ the sun went dark, the sacred curtain of the Temple was rent, the earth itself quaked, and tombs released their dead (Mt 27:45–53).

22. Ps 98.

23. Rom 8:19–23.

24. Is 34, for example, speaks of the healing of humanity and nature in one act.

25. Gn 3:20.

26. Gn 6:10.

27. Lk 21.

28. Ps 65:11–13.

29. Peter Brown, *Augustine of Hippo: A Biography* (Berkeley: University of California Press, 1969), 86.

30. Ibid., 84.

31. St. Ambrose, *Creation*, in *Creation, Paradise, Cain and Abel*, trans. John Savage (New York: Fathers of the Church, 1961), 252.

32. Brown, *Augustine*, 85.

33. Ibid., 84.

34. St. Ambrose, *Creation*, 6.

35. Ibid., 69.

36. Ibid., 67.

37. Ibid., 70.

зо. Ibid., 104–6.

39. Ibid., 96.

40. Ibid., 277.

41. Ibid., 256.

42. Ibid., 282.

43. Ibid., 35. "Evil is not a substance, but an accident, a deviation from the goodness of nature" (ibid., 32).

44. Brown, *Augustine*, 154.

45. Margaret Miles, *Fullness of Life: Historical Foundations for a New Asceticism* (Philadelphia: Westminster Press, 1981), 77.

46. Ibid., 68. George Lindbeck in his *The Nature of Doctrine* (Philadelphia: Westminster Press, 1984), 86, uses the soul-body dualism as an example of how within a particular anthropology the immortality of the soul makes sense and is true while not being clearly compatible with Hebrew and modern conceptions of the human person.

47. Robin Lane Fox, *Pagans and Christians* (New York: Alfred A. Knopf, 1987), 544.

48. St. Ambrose, *De excessu fratris sui*, bk. 1 (PL 16, 1354).

49. Erich Auerbach, *Mimesis: The Representation of Reality in Western Literature* (Garden City, NY: Doubleday, 1957), 19.

Chapter 5: Genesis Applied by Pope John Paul II

1. John Paul II, *Laborem exercens* ("On Human Labor," 1981), no. 4.

2. John Paul II, *Redemptor hominis* ("The Redeemer of Humanity," 1979), no. 14.

3. Ibid., no. 15. Here John Paul is echoing Paul VI's *Evangelii nuntiandi* ("On Evangelization," 1975), where Paul notes the "profound links" between the preaching of the Gospel on human advancement. Paul says they are of three orders: *anthropological* (referring to the historical existence of humanity), *theological* (because the plan of creation and the plan of redemption cannot be separated) and *evangelical* ("for how can we proclaim the new commandment to love without promoting justice?") (no. 31).

4. Paul VI, *Populorum progressio* ("On the Progress of Peoples," 1967), no. 76.

5. John Paul II, *Sollicitudo rei socialis* ("Concern for Social Matters," 1987), no. 8.

6. Andre Frossard *N'ayez pas peur! Dialogue avec Jean-Paul II* (Paris: Robert Laffont, 1982), 20–21.

7. Ibid., 22.

8. Ibid., 42.

9. Ibid., 39.

10. John Carmody, *Ecology and Religion* (New York: Paulist Press, 1983), 5–6.

11. John Paul II, *Dives in misericordia* ("Rich in Mercy," 1980), no. 1.

12. *Redemptor hominis*, no. 9.

13. Gn 1.

14. Rm 8:19–22.

15. *Redemptor hominis*, no. 8.

16. Ibid., no. 9.

17. Ibid., no. 10.

18. John Paul II, *Original Unity of Man and Woman: Catechesis on the Book of Genesis* (Boston: St. Paul Editions, 1981), 73, etc.

19. Kari Elisabeth Borresen, letter to the author, Oslo, 5 December 1987. See her *Subordination and Equivalence: The Nature and Role of Women in Augustine and Thomas Aquinas* (Washington, DC: University Press of America, 1981). In his apostolic letter *Mulieris dignitatem* ("On the Dignity of Women") of 15 August 1988, John Paul II sees the subjection of women to men not as a natural condition but as part of the heritage of sin (no. 10).

20. *Laborem exercens*, no. 3.

21. Gn 1:26.

22. Gn 1:28.

23. *Laborem exercens*, no. 4.

24. Ibid., no. 3.

25. Ibid., no. 4.

26. Ibid., no. 6.

27. Ibid., no. 12–13.

28. Ibid., no. 9.

29. Ibid., no. 14.

30. Ibid., no. 1.

31. Claus Westermann, *Genesis* (Grand Rapids: Wm. B. Eerdmans, 1987), 11.

32. Gregory Baum, *The Priority of Labor* (New York: Paulist Press, 1982), 36.

33. *Populorum progressio*, no. 3.

34. *Sollicitudo*, no. 26.
35. Ibid., no. 34.
36. Gn 2:16–17.
37. *Sollicitudo*, no. 34.
38. Ibid., no. 30.
39. Ibid.
40. Ibid.
41. Ibid., no. 38.
42. *Sollicitudo*, no. 29.
43. Cardinal Josef Hoffner, "The World Economy in the Light of Catholic Social Teaching," *Communio*, Fall 1986, 205–15.
44. *Sollicitudo*, no. 29–30.
45. Ibid., no. 37.
46. Ibid., no. 46.
47. Ibid., no. 38.
48. Ibid., no. 40.
49. William Safire, *New York Times*, 22 February 1988, Section A.
50. *Redemptor hominis*, no. 16.
51. *Sollicitudo*, no. 28.
52. Ibid., no. 10.
53. *Populorum progressio*, nos. 22–23.
54. See John Finnis, *Natural Law and Natural Rights* (Oxford: Clarendon Press, 1977), 155.
55. *Laborem exercens* nos. 14, 19.
56. Berman, *Law and Revolution*, 28–41.
57. *Sollicitudo*, no. 38.

58. Congregation for the Doctrine of the Faith, "Instruction on Respect for Human Life in its Origin and on the Dignity of Procreation," in *Origins* 16, no. 40 (19 March 1987): 3.

59. Joseph Sittler, *Essays on Nature and Grace* (Philadelphia: Fortress Press, 1971), 16.

60. Edward O. Wilson, *On Human Nature* (Cambridge: Harvard University Press, 1978), 141–42.

61. James M. Gustafson, *Theology and Ethics* (Oxford: Basil Blackwell, 1981), 20.

62. William A. Luijpen, *Phenomenology of Natural Law* (Pittsburgh: Duquesne University Press, 1967), 144, 242. These observations may strike some as too irenic, given the continuing discussion about natural law. To make such a re-evaluation credible today, it is necessary to avoid the natural law's traditional connotations of an ahistorical objectivism. Two poles must be kept in mind: that of limit ("nature") and that of transcendence (which is person taken both as human transcendence and as part of the historical process). See Vincent MacNamara, *Faith and Ethics* (Washington, DC: Georgetown University Press, 1985); Richard Bernstein, *Beyond Objectivism and Relativism* (Philadelphia: University of Pennsylvania Press, 1983); and Finnis, *Natural Law and Natural Rights*, 260–96.

63. See Roger Heckel, S.J., *General Aspects of the Social Catechesis of John Paul II* (Vatican City: Pontifical Commission Justitia et Pax, 1980), 16–18.

64. Lloyd L. Weinreb, *Natural Law and Justice* (Cambridge: Harvard University Press, 1987), 12.

65. See Neal Acherson, "The Death Doctors," *New York Review of Books* 34, no. 9, (28 May 1987): 29–34.

66. Wis 9:1–6.

67. Baum, *The Priority of Labor*, 32.

68. *Sollicitudo*, no. 47.

69. John Paul II, "Message for the World Day of Peace," 1 January 1987, no. 2.

70. Michael Collins, *Our Universe* (Washington, DC: National Geographic Society, 1980), foreword.

Chapter 6: Humilitas

1. Heb 11:13–16.

2. 1 Pt 1:9, 2:11.

3. 2 Pt 3:13 ("What we are waiting for, relying on his promises, is the new heavens and new earth, where uprightness will be at home"). See also Is 60:21; 65:17; 66:22.

4. Rv 21:2.

5. Cited by Ernst Pawel, *The Nightmare of Reason: A Life of Franz Kafka* (New York: Vintage Books, 1985), 191.

6. Ibid., 44.

7. Franz Kafka, *The Trial* (New York: Vintage Books, 1969), 3.

8. Pawel, *The Nightmare of Reason*, 19.

9. Ibid., 409.

10. Diaries, 1914–23, cited by Michel Carrouges, *Kafka vs. Kafka.*, trans. Emmet Parker (University, AL: University of Alabama Press, 1968), 213–14.

11. Ibid., 119.

12. Eleanor Munro, *On Glory Roads* (New York: Thames and Hudson, 1987), 126.

13. Ibid., 232.

14. Ibid., 4.

15. Ibid., 232.

16. Annie Dillard, *An American Childhood* (New York: Harper and Row, 1987), 3.

17. Ibid., 135.

18. Ibid., 248–49.

19. Ibid., 249.

20. Annie Dillard, *Teaching a Stone to Talk* (New York: Harper and Row, 1982), 69.

21. See Ps 87: "It is he, the Lord, who gives each his place."

22. Walter Brueggemann, *The Land* (Philadelphia: Fortress Press, 1977), 187.

23. Lk 9:58.

24. Simone Petrement, *Simone Weil: A Life* (New York: Pantheon Books, 1976), 396.

25. Simone Weil, *Gateway to God* (London: Collins, 1974), 41 ff.

26. Munro, *Glory Roads*, 73.

27. See Pheme Perkins, *Resurrection: New Testament Witness and Contemporary Reflection* (Garden City, NY: Doubleday, 1984), 25. She asserts, correctly, that resurrection is of the same theological order as the creation itself.

28. See Acts 17:32. Similarly, Simone Weil: "The cross is sufficient for me" (*Gateway to God*, 33).

29. 1 Cor 15:20.

30. Rv 21:5.

31. 1 Cor 36–38.

32. Mt 22:23–33.

33. Rm 8:23.

34. Nancy Gauthier, "Les images de l'au-delà durant l'antiquité chrétienne," *Revue des Études Augustiniennes* 33, no. 1: 4.

35. Mk 11:17.

36. Is 56:7.

37. Conor Cruise O'Brien, *God Land: Reflections on Religion and Nationalism* (Cambridge: Harvard University Press, 1988), 4.

38. Ibid., 7.

39. See Walter Brueggemann, "Land: Fertility and Justice," in *Theology of the Land*, ed. Bernard Evans and Gregory Cusack (Collegeville: Liturgical Press, 1987), 41–68.

40. John Paul II, *Sollicitudo*, no. 48, citing *Gaudium et spes*, no. 39.

41. *Gaudium et spes*, no. 42.

42. *Presbyterorum ordinis*, no. 3.

43. Michel Carrouges, *Kafka vs. Kafka*, 9.

44. Mk 12:27.

45. 1 Cor 1:15:28.

46. Czeslaw Milosz, *The Collected Poems* (New York: Ecco Press, 1988), 455.

47. Arendt, *The Human Condition*, 315–316.

48. Gn 28:12–17.

49. Jn 1:51.
50. Mt 27:50.
51. Jn 20:15.
52. 1 Pt 1:13.
53. Mt 5:5.
54. 1 Pt 1:10.
55. 1 Pt 3:8.
56. 1 Pt 4:8–10, 5: 5.

INDEX

Adam, xii, 88, 92, 132, 142
Alienation, 3, 19–20, 129–131
Ammons, A. R., 70–71
Animals
  in art, 105
  genetically patented, 40
  human naming of, 93
  as human property, 25–26, 40, 115
  intrinsic value of, 79, 101
  killing of, 37–38, 89, 93
  legal protection of, 39–40
  preservation issues, 10, 40
  rights, 25
  sharing earth with, 37–38, 115
Anthropocentrism, 92, 109
Apocalyptic beliefs, 16–18
Aquinas, Thomas, 122
Arendt, Hannah, xvii, 19, 141
Aristotelianism, 46

Art and nature
  apocalyptic imagery, 17
  the Hudson River school, 64–65
  nature morte, 95
  Ravenna's church mosaics, 105
  the Sistine Chapel, xii
  St. Peter's, 142–144

Barth, Karl, 80
Berman, Harold J., 22, 121
Bible, the
  interpretation of, 61–62
  materiality and spirituality of, 104–105
  as revelation, 56
  as a source for ethics, 53–58
  See also Book of Genesis
Biology, 9–10, 40
Blake, William, 55–56

171

Bloom, Harold, 55
Book of Genesis, xi–xii
  and contemporary
    environmental concerns,
    84–98
  cosmology and, 52–53
  creation and redemption,
    86–88
  creation stories, 88–91
  on earth as home, 6
  St. Ambrose on, 99–105
Brown, Peter, 102–103
Bruegemann, Walter, 134

Canaan, 94–95, 131–132,
    138, 160
  religion of, 87–88
Carson, Rachel, 37–39
Catholic church, the
  Biblical interpretation and,
    61–62
  the church/world
    relationship, 23–24
  churches, 18–19, 142–143
  religion and science and,
    47–48, 52–53, 65–74
  social teachings of, 2, 107,
    140
    on global issues, 7–8
    the next step, 21–26
    Pope Leo XIII and, 23
  See also Pope Leo XIII
Charity, 21, 109
Chesterton, G. K., 28–29
Christ, 2, 63, 69–71, 105, 126

  resurrection of, 69, 104,
    136
  See also Jesus of Nazareth
Christianity blamed for
    environmental crisis,
    74–75
Christology, 44, 53, 75
Church and state, 22–23
Cobb, John, 66, 73–75, 78,
    81–83
Collins, Michael, 127
Common good, 118
  definitions of, 10–12, 120–
    121
  public vs. private, 42, 113,
    120
  tragedy of the commons,
    11–12
Communion with God, 3,
    118
Communion of the sexes, 112
"Concern for Social Matters."
    See under Encyclical
Conservation biology, 40
Conservationists, 33–37
Contraception, 13–14
Cosmology, 19–20, 49–53,
    67, 115
  "big bang" creation theory,
    50–51
Creation
  admiration of, 101–102
  creation theology and, 54,
    76
  in Genesis, 83, 89

goodness of, 89–90
nature as, 26
St. Ambrose on, 99–105
theology of, xiv, 54, 76, 82
and scientific theory,
  50–51
See also Human dominion
  over creation
Creed, The, 4

Darwin, Charles, 44, 48, 64–
  65, 67
De Lubac, Henri, 69–70
Development
human, 107, 116, 119
land, 95
third-world, 39, 78, 107
Dickinson, Emily, 156
Dillard, Annie, 133–134
Divorce, 83

Earth
exploitation of the, 14, 41–
  42, 92
as God-forsaken, 77–78
heaven on, 29, 138–139,
  147–148
"house rules" for, 129,
  140–144
and "subdue the earth"
  interpretations, 75, 94–
  95, 113, 120
See also Land
Eastern religions, x, 132–
  133, 135

Ecology, 8, 129, 146
Economics, 9–10, 35–36, 117
capitalism, 78, 108–109,
  119
consumerism and
  materialism, 118–119
living standards, 7–8
Marxist collectivism, 108,
  125
Pope John Paul II on, 108,
  113, 125
Eliade, Mircea, 27
Encyclical
definition of, 107
Laborem exercens ("On
  Human Labor," 1981),
  108, 111–114, 121
Mater et Magistra
  ("Mother and Teacher,"
  1961), 91, 122
Populorum progressio
  ("On the Progress of
  Peoples," 1967), 107
Redemptor hominis ("The
  Redeemer of Humanity,"
  1979), 107–108, 110–
  111
Rerum novarum ("Of New
  Things," 1891), 23, 91,
  112
Solicitudo rei socialis
  ("Concern for Social
  Matters," 1987), 106–
  107, 115–127
Environmental concerns,

Pope John Paul II on,
114–115
Environmental ethic. *See
under* Ethics
Environmental impact
assessments, 32, 38, 43
Environmental movement
ambiguity of, 32
elitism of, xv, 30–31, 34
impact of, xiv–xv, 30, 37
optimistic conservationists,
33–37
pessimistic
environmentalists, 37–
42
politics and the, 32–33
Eschatology, 53, 63, 76
Ethics
natural law and, 123–126
need for environmental, 7–
15
philosophy and science
and, 58–63
specificity of Christian,
58–63
Eve, 96–97
Evolution, xiv, 69–71
Christogenesis and, 68
goal of, 76
See also Creation; Science
Exploitation of the planet. *See
under* Earth

Faith, xvii–xviii, 61, 72, 135
reason and, 48, 50–51
Flood, the, 93

Fox, Robin Lane, 103–104
Frye, Northrop, 55–56
Fuchs, Josef, 59–62

Galeazzi, Enrico, 142
Gaudium et spes ("On the
Church in the World of
Today"), 80, 107
on the church/world
relationship, 24
on ethics and scientific
advances, 71–73
See also Vatican Council II
Genetics, 40, 44
Gilson, Etienne, 46–47
Global moral issues, 7–8,
116–117
the environment, 23, 32–
33, 39, 114–115
living standards disparity,
7–8
nuclear threat, 7–8, 16–
17, 31–32, 37, 111
universal distribution of
earthly goods, 35–36,
117
Governmental issues, 10–12,
22–23, 38–40, 91–92
politics and, 9–10, 32
Greek antiquity, xvii, 95–96,
136
Greek Fathers, 99
Greenpeace, 32

Hardin, Garret, 11–12
Hartshorne, Charles, 78–79

Hawking, Stephen W., 50–51
Heaven on earth, 29, 138–139, 147–148
Home
  earthly existence as, xii–xiv, 1–7, 45, 54, 127
  of God, 2–3, 6
  the search for a, 54, 130–132
Hope, xvii–xviii, 76–77, 135, 137, 139, 141
Hotel
  earthly existence as a, xiii–xiv, 57–58, 130
Human dominion over creation, 89, 92–98, 114–115, 118
  anthropocentrism, 92, 109
  and "subdue the earth" interpretations, 75, 94–95, 113, 120
  waste and, 39, 119
  See also Animals
Human global responsibility. See Stewardship of creation
"Human Labor, On." See under Encyclical
Human person
  admirable qualities of, 101–102
  dignity of, 91–92, 107, 111
  idea of, 46
  as imago Dei, 53, 78, 88–92, 102, 112–113, 115–116, 124, 126

organ donation, 41
Pope John Paul II on the, 111–114
rights of, 91–92
Human soul, 102, 162
Human work and self-actualization, 112–114
Humility and other virtues, 140–144

Industrialization, 10, 23, 27, 111, 115
Israel, religion of, 18, 86–88, 160

Jesus of Nazareth, 5, 63, 70, 137
  See also Christ
John Paul II. See Pope John Paul II
Judaism, 61–62, 70, 77, 96, 133, 136, 138–139
  Amos and, 57–58
  Yiddish literature, 62
Judeo-Christian tradition, xv, 18, 26
Justice, 21, 109, 113
  See also Global moral issues
Justin Martyr, 20

Kafka, Franz, 129
Kantian philosophy, 81–82
Kaufman, Gordon, 81
Kiss, the, 101–102, 127
Kubrick, Stanley, 17

Labor. *See* Work
Land
  divine gift of, 94, 97, 135
  ethic development, 35, 41–
    42, 139
  as property, 35–36
  the subduing of, 76, 94–
    95, 113, 120
  See also Earth
Land of Promise, 132–140
Land, the Promised, 86–87,
  129, 131–132, 138
Lazarus, 118–119
Legal issues, 10–12, 22–23
  environmental legislation,
    38–40
  Pope John Paul II on
    natural law, 117, 121–
    127
Leopold, Aldo, 34
Lifton, Robert Jay, 124–125
Lindbergh, Anne Morrow, 29

Maguire, David, 12
Materialism, 118–119
Men and women, 13, 83, 88,
  91–92, 95, 112, 136, 164
Metz, Johann Baptist, 74
Miles, Margaret, 103
Moltmann, Jürgen, 66, 75–
  78, 82
Moral universe, 54–57
Moses, 87–88, 99–100
"Mother and Teacher." *See*
  under Encyclical

Muir, John, 33–34
Munro, Eleanor, 132–133

Nationalism, 12, 138–139
Nature, 9, 88
  aliveness of, 95–96
  art and, xii, 64–65, 95, 105
  exploitation of, 14, 39, 41–
    42, 92, 115
  as God-forsaken, 77–78
  inanimate of, 93, 115
  integrity of, 47
  Pope John Paul II on
    natural law, 117, 121–
    127
  theology and, 81–83
  See also Creation; Property
Neoplatonism. *See under*
  Platonism
New Testament, the, 5, 61,
  136
Newton, Sir Isaac, 50, 52, 95
Noah, 27, 93, 97
nuclear threat, 7–8, 16–17,
  31–32, 37, 111

O'Brien, Conor Cruise, 138
"Of New Things." *See under*
  Encyclical
Old Testament, the, 27, 83,
  138–139
  See also Book of Genesis
Olmsted, Frederick Law, 33
Ozick, Cynthia, 62

Pantheism, 7, 69, 79, 134
Parks, 33–34
Pascal, Blaise, 65–67
Pastoral constitution. *See Gaudium et spes*
Patristic ideology, 53, 62
Peaceable kingdom, the, 93–94
Percy, Walker, 31
Personhood. *See Human person*
Philosophy
    ethics and, 58–63
    religion and science and, 45–53
Pilgrimage, 88, 132–134
Planet. *See Earth*
Platonism, 2, 4, 46, 90, 99–100, 134–135
    Neoplatonist ideology, 4, 103
Political issues, 9–10, 32–33
Pollution, 12, 37
    legislation, 38–40
    Pope John Paul II on, 111, 114–115
Pope Gregory VII, 22
Pope Leo XIII,
    Rerum novarum, 23, 91, 112
Pope John XXIII,
    Mater et Magistra, 91, 122
Pope Paul VI,
    Populorum progressio 107, 114, 120, 163

Pope John Paul II
    author's acquaintance with, xvi
    background of, xvii
    on creation, 50–51
    pre-1988 allusions to Genesis, 109–114
    environmental concerns of, 114–115
    on the fair distribution of goods, 119–121
    Humanae vitae, 12–14
    Laborem exercens, 108, 111–114, 121
    on natural law, 117, 121–127
    Redemptor hominis, 107–108, 110–111
    Solicitudo rei socialis, 106–107, 115–127
    on solidarity, 113, 117–119
    on suffering, 80
    See also Catholic church
Population growth, 12–14, 38
Preservation of animals, 10, 39–40, 79, 89, 115
Progress and the future, 15, 72–73, 78, 111, 116
"Progress of Peoples, On the."
    See under Encyclical
Property
    divine gift of land and, 97
    Pope John Paul II on, 108–109, 119–121

rights, 23, 35, 42, 121
  the common good and,
    10–12, 113, 120
  universal destination of all
    things and, 36, 113,
    119–121
Protestantism
  approaches to ethics and
    science, 47, 50, 74–81
  conservationism and, 35
  the Reformation, xi, 74–78
    (passim)
Psalms, 97–98

Reason
  faith and, 48, 50–51
  moral norms and, 59–60,
    124
  natural law and, 117, 121–
    127
"Redeemer of Humanity,
  The." See under
  Encyclical
Reformation, Protestant, xi,
  74–76 (passim)
Religion
  meaning of, 5–6
  philosophy and, 45–53
  science and, 45–53, 64–66
  science and Catholic, 65–
    74
  science and Protestant, 66,
    74–81
  warfare and, 138
Research and faith, 72

Revelation, 47–48, 62
Russell, Bertrand, 53–54

Sacramental consciousness,
  26–29
Salvation, 2, 15–22, 137
Santmire, Paul, 75
Schumacher, E. F., ix–x, 141
Science
  Catholic approaches to,
    65–74
  ethics and, 58–63
  the practice of, 9, 43
  Protestant approaches to,
    66, 74–81
  religion and philosophy
    and, 45–53
Secularity of the baptized,
  140
Secularization, Western, 26
Separation of powers, 22–23
Sin, 15, 86, 102, 116, 118,
  137
Sittler, Joseph, 66, 75–76
Smith, Adam, 11
Solicitudo rei socialis
    ("Concern for Social
    Matters")
  fair distribution of goods,
    119–121
  the natural law, 121–127
  solidarity principle, 113,
    117–119
  See also under encyclical
Solomon, 125

Space and the universe. *See* Cosmology
Spirituality, 20–21
State, human precedence over the, 91–92
Stewardship of creation, 3, 22, 33, 52, 146
  animals and the, 25–26, 37, 89, 115
  See also Human dominion over creation
St. Ambrose on Genesis, 4, 99–105
St. Augustine, xi, 49, 98–99, 102–103, 112
St. Paul, 69–70, 136
  Letter to the Romans, 82, 96, 110–111
St. Peter, 143–144
"Subdue the earth." *See* Human dominion over creation
Surrelativism, 79–80

Teilhard de Chardin, Pierre, 44, 65–73, 79
Theocentrism, 109
Theology, 45–48
  classical theism, 78–80
  creation, 54, 76
  history and, 74
  liberation, 73
  nature and, 81–83
  political, 73–74, 76
  process, 49, 73–76, 78–81

Thurow, Lester, xv
Tillich, Paul, 27–28, 82
Tragedy of the commons, 11–12
Trinity, the divine, 77

U. S. Environmental Protection Agency (E. P. A.), 38
U. S. Patent and Trademark Office, 40
United Nations Conference on the Human Environment (1972), 9

Vatican Council II, 83, 107, 109, 140
  on earthly goods' universal destination, 36
  on ethics and scientific advances, 71–73
  on the world, 15–16
  See also Gaudium et spes
Virtues, theological, 140–144
Voegelin, Eric, 19–20

Walzer, Michael, 54–56, 61
Ward, Barbara, 8–9
Water and the seas, 12, 27, 100
White, Lynn, Jr., 74–75
Whitehead, Alfred North, 76, 78–79, 140
Williams, Bernard, 60
Wilson, Edward O., 43–45

Women and men, 13, 83, 88, 91–92, 95, 112, 136, 164
Work
  Pope John Paul II on, 112–114
World
  end of the, 16–18
    interpretations of the, 15–20
    this passing, 15–16

Yahweh, 86–88, 134
Yourcenar, Marguerite, 28